THE FINAL
TRUTH

Uncovering the Illusions of Your Reality

JUSTIN BOYNTON

Contents

Overview

Amid the digital age, social media bursts with countless voices claiming authority on life's most significant questions. What unfolds is a confusion, a mix of beliefs fighting for dominance. From spirituality to the controversy of psychedelics, to the mysteries of God and death, the landscape is filled with diverse opinions. But why does the truth seem so elusive, buried beneath an avalanche of perspectives?

If you've ever questioned the chaos, or just the basic meaning of life, this book is your lifeline. Within these pages, a profound journey awaits. One that not only uncovers the hidden truths behind life's important questions, but also teaches you how to sift through the noise and discern what is the truth. Prepare to embark on a transformational expedition, requiring an open heart and mind to embrace the revelations that await within. As the fog of uncertainty lifts, clarity emerges, guiding you toward a more profound understanding of the world and your place in it.

Introduction

The Truth. What is it? What does it truly signify? Is your truth the same as mine? Is an Atheist's truth synonymous with a Christian's? Does the truth of a pessimist align with that of an optimist? Does a conservative's truth mirror a liberal's? What one person is conscious of, another may remain unconscious to. And what about the collective consciousness? Does truth live within it? What truth does spirituality hold?

Imagine if everything you held as knowledge, your perceived reality, was in fact a falsehood. What if it was a deceptive illusion or a comfortable convenience that you clung to, simply to sustain your personal comprehension of this world? What if an Atheist discovered the existence of a higher power? Or if a Christian realized the influence of darkness that influences their thoughts and actions? What if a liberal saw what they believed to be unwavering truth was, in reality, a mere smokescreen? And what if a conservative uncovered their convictions had been subtly tainted for a hidden agenda?

As you delve into the contents of this book, you might encounter resistance, inner conflict, the urge to retreat, or even an absolute inability to accept certain truths. Some will find themselves taken aback, tempted to abruptly close the book and distance themselves from its contents. Why is this? A single word holds the answer: consciousness. Our consciousness shapes our capacity to embrace or discard ideas. For example, an atheist discussing the seemingly preposterous notion of a divine presence with a fellow atheist will find comfort and acceptance within their shared consciousness.

Similarly, those immersed in spiritual contemplation engage in conversations with like-minded individuals, discussing spiritual guides, sagging rituals, and ancestral connections. They ground their conversations in a shared level of consciousness, making it easier to accept personal realities regarding beliefs and subjects.

Now, consider the concept of a singular Truth. A Truth that remains unaltered regardless of individual perspectives or the affiliations of various groups. This Truth stands unwavering amidst the fluidity of beliefs, encompassing God, spirituality, empaths, psychedelics, darkness, and Death. This Truth is the cornerstone of the revelations awaiting you within these pages. Welcome the challenge of staying engaged throughout the entire journey. It will undoubtedly become demanding, but within this struggle lies the potential for profound growth and understanding. What you find here will change your reality and the life you live today.

Beginning with Understanding

We must grasp the concept of consciousness in order to comprehend what lies ahead in this book. Let's start with the basics briefly before delving into the truth of our existence. When you encounter a truth and feel a strong resistance welling up within you, it's crucial to understand its origin and reason. This understanding is essential for you to continue learning the truth. Let's look at a couple of definitions really quick.

Consciousness; refers to the state of being aware of one's thoughts, feelings, sensations, and surroundings. It encompasses the awareness and perception of both the external environment and one's internal mental and emotional experiences. Consciousness allows individuals to engage in self-reflection, make decisions, and experience subjective phenomena, such as emotions and thoughts. It is considered a fundamental aspect of human experience and is closely intertwined with the sense of self and individual identity. Consciousness can range from everyday awareness to altered states of consciousness, such as during meditation, dreams, or other transformative experiences.

Unconsciousness; pertains to a state of being unaware or lacking conscious understanding. It signifies a lack of recognition or comprehension of information or concepts. In this state, the mind is not actively processing or engaging with thoughts, ideas, or external stimuli, resulting in a lack of conscious awareness or cognitive engagement.

Now that we have clarified the definitions, please fetch a piece of paper and a pen. Yes, go ahead and get them; we'll wait. Ready? Draw the largest circle possible on that sheet of paper. Imagine, within that circle, all knowledge of the universe exists. This encompasses all knowledge from the inception of Earth until the present day. It includes knowledge about space, stars, planets, and everything on Earth. It captures the entirety of humanity's history and discoveries. Everything known in the universe lives within that circle.

Now, you're going to draw a second circle, but before you do, you need to understand its representation. You will draw this second circle inside the first one. The second circle will symbolize your personal knowledge of the universe. This encompasses everything you have learned about space, planets, and our Earth. It includes knowledge spanning from the beginning of time until the present day. Also, it encompasses everything you are aware of and possess knowledge about. Go ahead and draw your circle of knowledge within the universe.

If anyone drew more than a dot, the smallest mark a pen or pencil can make, well, I won't judge, but there might be some introspective work in your future. Regardless, whatever you have drawn is acceptable. The second circle, your circle, represents what you know and understand about the universe. The space between the outer boundary of your circle and the first circle represents uncharted territory. It symbolizes the realm of the unconscious.

As you progress through this book, a process will unfold in which we draw additional circles just outside your initial one. Whether these circles connect and your sphere of knowledge expands will entirely depend on you. Can you embrace the truth as it is, or do you dismiss it? It might take days, weeks, or even months for you to fully grasp the truth. For some, full understanding may not occur until the threshold of death.

Between Light and Darkness:
My Path to The Truth

In the innocence of childhood, I welcomed God into my life at a remarkably tender age, just five years old. One Sunday morning, my parents brought me to a local church. When the pastor inquired whether anyone sought God's presence in their life, I eagerly conveyed my desire to my parents. Even then, I sensed a deep connection to God and yearned to be enveloped by His presence. Throughout my adolescent years, this bond grew stronger.

My devotion took me to a church retreat in my late teens, where I was one of the youth leaders for the weekend. During a soul-stirring evening of singing, a burning sensation ignited within my chest, an unfamiliar but undeniable sensation. Amid the singing, a voice revealed to me, "He struggles with pornography." Though surrounded by many youths, I immediately recognized the subject of the message.

Embarrassment held me prisoner. Bringing up the topic of pornography with the youth in question appeared unthinkable. Despite the undeniable power resonating within my chest, doubt crept in. What if I misunderstood the message? What if my words brought humiliation upon the young person and me? Overwhelmed by embarrassment, I silenced the message. Deep down, I understood God's intent to guide and aid the struggling youth; yet I failed to act on it. Subsequently, an overwhelming guilt became my unwavering companion, haunting me for three decades. A promise took root deep within me: if granted a second chance, I would not fail to deliver

God's message again. It would be the last time I received a message from God for nearly 30 years.

Throughout my adult life, I wandered from place to place. Yet I always carried the awareness of God's presence, sporadically engaging in heartfelt prayer. The dialogue remained one-sided; me vocalizing my thoughts and feelings, while His responses remained silent. Following my failure to relay His message to that youth, His voice seemed to retreat into silence.

In my mid-forties, I became tired and burdened by life. It was heavy. I began looking for answers, an escape from the weight I was carrying. I embarked on a journey with psychedelic mushrooms. This venture proved transformative. I was living outside the US, and it was an incredible experience for me. I saw rejection, abandonment, abuse, insecurity, etc., and started removing it all from my body.

As I cleared away the darkness within, I grew increasingly sensitive to everything around me. This newfound sensitivity to other people perplexed me until a friend proposed a fitting label: 'empath.' I did not know what being an "empath" meant. Intrigued, I decided to look up this term, and a striking revelation emerged, all of my life-long experiences perfectly aligned with the description of an empath.

Not long after making this discovery, a woman came knocking at my door. She introduced herself as Susan, a self-proclaimed witch who practiced only white magic. Susan explained that white magic was focused on helping people. She had learned her skills from someone who had been involved in black magic. This person had aided drug traffickers for years and was now dealing with a terminal brain tumor in her early 50s.

Susan sensed something special within me. She mentioned the presence of my guardian angel, describing it as the largest she had ever encountered. In her view, my potential surpassed her own, and she extended an offer to mentor me in harnessing this newfound power to assist others. To my astonishment, she revealed private details about my life that nobody else could have known, validating her abilities. Her remarkable insights delved into my past and provided guidance to steer clear of potential problems in the upcoming days.

Susan introduced me to spiritual guides and ancestral influences that navigate us. She employed sage, lit candles to saints of the Catholic Church, and purged bad energy. I can still vividly recall the first time I heard a guiding voice. During an evening walk, the voice directed me, saying, 'Stop, look at that family over there.' I hadn't even noticed the family through the trees. The voice was tender yet guiding. 'Observe how that family bonds and establishes connections. That's an aspect you lacked while growing up. That's why you feel uncomfortable in family situations. The voice provided counsel on fostering connections with family and others.

I had previously walked closely with God, tangibly feeling His presence. Yet, confusion clouded my perception. This unfolding reality was undeniable. I was growing increasingly spiritual, yet an isolating feeling emerged. How could this be? I questioned. How could I possess such profound connections to the spiritual realm and yet not sense God's nearness? Then, a second spiritual guide emerged from within, a rapid conversationalist. To my surprise, Susan confirmed that we both had the same spiritual guide, pointing out his quick speech patterns, a detail I hadn't previously shared with her. This validation of my experiences added a solid layer of authenticity to what I was encountering.

One day, Susan came over, visibly distressed, and struggled to share a revelation she had received from her spiritual guide. She had confirmed it multiple times through various means, including tarot cards, and her guides had consistently confirmed its truth. Finally, she mustered the courage to break the news to me.

Susan explained her spiritual guides had confirmed something groundbreaking: my father, the one who had raised me, was not my biological father. Upon hearing this news, I was both distressed and strangely relieved. It suddenly explained so much about our strained relationship and the abuse I had endured from him, which my other siblings had been spared. However, I needed to be sure.

I called my mother, who insisted that my father was indeed my biological father. She even expressed that she would have been relieved if it had been someone else because she empathized deeply with what I had gone through as a child.

I then contacted my brother and asked him to do a sibling DNA test with me, even though he found it silly. Given that I was living in another country, it took four long weeks to organize everything and receive the test results. Those weeks were agonizing, filled with uncertainty about whether my entire life had been a lie. Susan even conducted readings during that time, and each time, they confirmed the shocking revelation. The spiritual forces seemed unshakably certain they knew the truth.

Finally, the DNA results arrived. After four weeks of anticipation and the belief that they would validate what the guides had said, I opened the envelope. As I read through the numbers, it became undeniably clear: my brother and I shared the same maternal and paternal DNA. It left me utterly speechless. How could this be? I thought. How could these so-called "guides" have been so wrong and turned my life upside down like this?

Then, a crucial moment arrived. During an introspective session, a commanding voice declared, *"They are lying and deceiving you."* The resonance of that voice was unmistakable. I had felt it once before, back during the youth retreat nearly 30 years ago. The presence was both powerful and undeniable. In that instant, a veil was lifted from my eyes, and I saw darkness infiltrating me. I suddenly saw, and fully realized all at once, that the "spiritual guides" and "ancestors" were actually demons, cleverly disguised as helpers.

The realization was strikingly simple in its profundity. The truth: There is only God and there is only Satan. Yet we look to sagging rituals, candles, stones, the universe and nature to replace God. These diversions were cunning tactics to divert us, God's children, from the unadulterated truth. By ever so slightly altering our trajectory, they could redirect our destination entirely.

God had concealed the truth about my father from the demons. They believed they could manipulate me with the revelation that he wasn't my biological father. If they could convince me of their supernatural power through such a revelation, they could potentially gain control over me. However, God had different intentions. He exposed their lies and deception with an earth-shattering revelation. This is how God guided me back to the truth.

God intervened in my journey, shedding light on the darkness that had been clouding my understanding. He revealed the schemes of the enemy, the deceit and falsehoods designed to harm His beloved children. On that day, a profound revelation unfolded before me. Overcome with realization, I humbly knelt before God, seeking His forgiveness and guidance. With a wholehearted commitment, I vowed to carry out His will and offer my help in any way possible.

In that exact moment, on that very day, God gave me another message for someone, the friend who had introduced me to Susan. This message carried great power, and I felt a mixture of awe and fear at the prospect of delivering it. The familiar burning sensation in my chest erased any doubt about its source. I had made a firm resolve never to waver in conveying God's messages, no matter the potential consequences. Soon, my friend came to visit, and I delivered the message:

"Daughter of Satan. Why do you lead my people astray? I am the Creator of the Universe, God of the heavens and the earth; I do not use witchcraft to speak with my children. Turn from your wicked ways before it is too late. Return to your Father who created you and loves you."

With sweaty palms and a racing heart, I delivered that message. The words had repeated in my head a hundred times, word for word, until my friend arrived. Despite anticipating potential excommunication from her life after conveying such a powerful message, something unexpected occurred. The words I spoke resonated deeply within her heart. God doesn't solely rely on words; He also works in the person's heart.

Later, my friend would reveal that on that very day, Susan had contacted her, filled with concern. The shared spiritual guide had reportedly communicated that he must depart, ending his connection with both her and me. Another spiritual guide, a demon, had instructed Susan to inform my friend not to visit me on that day. These demons asserted I was confused and incapable of understanding their messages. They urged her to distance herself from me immediately. Without delay, Susan disappeared from my life, just as darkness flees from the light.

I began receiving more and more messages for people. No matter how embarrassed I was or how difficult it was, I delivered each and every one. Most would be images I would have to put into words, then a translation of the message, then God's guidance. One particularly powerful message depicted a vibrant garden, flourishing with thriving green plants. The sun shone brilliantly from above, illuminating the scene. However, as the plants grew taller, an encroaching darkness began to overshadow the once-vibrant greenery. The darkness engulfed the plants, gradually choking out the sunlight until only a faint sliver remained.

This specific message was meant for Mary, an older single woman whom I had briefly met six months prior. Despite my nervousness, there was no retreat. I had dedicated myself to convey all messages given to me by God. I reached out to her, asking if we could meet and talk. Upon arrival, my nerves were evident as I described the intricate vision that had unveiled itself before me. Slowly and cautiously, I gave her the interpretation.

"The green garden symbolizes your youth, a time when life was fresh and vibrant. The growing plants signify the passing years. However, with time, darkness has overshadowed the light that once filled your life. In the present day, only a slender glimmer of that light remains within you. This darkness, which has gradually accumulated over decades, gives rise to secondary effects within you, including unexplainable sadness and depression."

The message's impact resonated deeply within her. As for the guidance, God's intention was clear: to assist her in removing the darkness that had clouded her life and to once again embrace His light and love. Little did I know, the demons had also led astray this woman. She had opened the door to the spiritual realm by attending nature focused retreats, collecting spiritual stones, and lighting candles to saints of the Catholic Church. Despite her endeavors, none of these practices yielded fruit, as they were gradually pulling her away from the true source of light, God.

Face to Face:
My Startling Encounter with Darkness

I was contacted by someone named Jane, who had distanced herself from me a few months prior. She was grappling with something heavy, though she couldn't pinpoint it or comprehend how to manage it. By this point, I had begun to perceive the emotional burdens that people carried and helped them process or release these emotions. Until then, these burdens had been predominantly emotional and rooted in pain. God had guided me, emphasizing that I required a person's consent to connect with them, as the gift I had been given was invasive. It was never to be employed without the individual's consent. God respects our personal choices and free will to a degree that can be difficult to comprehend.

While meeting with Jane, I inquired about her feelings and the source of her struggle. She remained clueless. Seeking her permission to connect with her and gain insight, I was granted consent. After a few moments, I began perceiving a dark presence near her heart. In my attempt to understand it, I noticed a tube-like darkness extending downward towards her abdomen area. It was an intensely dark presence; unlike any I had encountered before. As I attempted to discern its nature, a realization struck me: it was a demon! This realization left me stunned; I had never seen one in another person before. I was at a loss regarding how to raise the subject with Jane casually. After all, how does one casually mention, "Hey, so I saw a demon inside you"?

Seeking not to alarm Jane, I instructed the demon to depart in the name of Jesus, a phrase ingrained from my early church attendance. To my surprise, the demon replied, "No." I was taken aback; I had assumed this approach would work, right? Undeterred, I repeated my command, "Get out in the name of Jesus!" Yet again, the response was a resolute, "No." The demon flat out told me that Jane had willingly invited its presence into her life and she was the only one capable of commanding it to leave.

"Well, that was a curveball," I thought. Now, I had to figure out how to inform Jane that I was having a conversation with a demon within her. At this point, Jane didn't know God. In fact, I wasn't even sure if she believed in God or Satan. The mind often struggles to comprehend and accept the spiritual aspects of this life, but I had to tell her the truth of what I was seeing. Clearing my throat and stumbling slightly, I mustered the courage to speak. "Um, so you have a demon, and he won't leave unless you tell him to," I sheepishly confessed to her.

Now in the story, I believe it's important to introduce two important words: "Somatic Release." At that point, I had only just started experiencing regular releases, physical manifestations like shaking, coughing, crying, or vomiting. This process aids in purging the darkness we carry within. Only a small percentage of people are capable of these releases in their day-to-day life. You can liken it to how a dog shakes during a thunderstorm when they are scared; they're releasing built-up nervous energy. Similarly, our bodies use this mechanism to release abuse trauma, darkness, and even demons. We are, after all, energy, and so is everything within us. The shaking or coughing serves as a release valve for what we harbor.

The gift God gave me is to facilitate releases for those who can't perform them. If someone carries intense negativity like hatred, which is exceedingly dark and heavy, I can connect with them and help release it through my own somatic experiences. We all share connections with one another, and as an empath, we form these connections at a much deeper level. During these connections, I can release on behalf of individuals who cannot do so themselves. This is why some individuals are often referred to as healers in this realm; they provide a path for another person's pain to escape.

So, getting back to Jane's story. Upon uttering those words, I began coughing and heaving, the release of the demon happening through me. At that moment, I wasn't fully aware of the precise details, but Jane later revealed that she had commanded the demon to leave when I informed her of what was transpiring. The will of a person to live with or without spiritual influence is a hallmark of the creation. As we have the freedom to choose God or not, we also have the freedom to choose the influence of darkness in our lives. This marked my initial experience in removing spiritual darkness from someone, the beginning of a brutal spiritual battle that would culminate in Satan ordering my death to prevent me from continuing God's work.

Not long after the experience with Jane, God granted me the authority to remove demons from individuals. Once I identified their presence within someone seeking help, I would issue a command for them to depart, and they would comply. In the weeks that followed, I had people showing up at my house daily. Sometimes I would have 2, 3, 4, or even 5 people waiting in the house for their turn. Word got out about how people were feeling afterward, and more and more individuals were hungry for God's healing. I could write several books about the spiritual struggles and the process of purging Satan's influence from a person. Indeed, what I came to understand was profoundly shocking to my consciousness.

Following Adam and Eve's consumption of the fruit from the tree of knowledge of good and evil, Satan found his way into the creation. A noteworthy aside is that God conveyed to me that while we often blame Adam and Eve for disrupting the creation, every subsequent human would have made the same choice as them. This insight explains why there has never been a full reset within the creation.

Many people perceive Satan's presence as some external mystical force. Just as God operates through the spirit, so does Satan. His influence lives within all of us. This inner presence shapes our decisions and thoughts. No one is exempt from it. Satan's influence remains an inherent part of us all within the creation. Ignoring this truth will not shield you from its influence.

As God continued removing darkness and expelling demons from people, the attacks began. Initially, some high-ranking demons of Satan tried to allure me with offers of money or possessions. When that failed, Satan himself approached me. Satan offered me whatever I desired. A million dollars? Done. An attractive partner? Done. Status? Done. He presented many enticements and implored me to aid him in dismantling the creation.

Over a span of around six months, I encountered no fewer than 30 such spiritual attacks. With each attempt to reach me, I had to consciously choose God, repeatedly affirming, "I choose God." I wondered why, during that season, God didn't shield me from these encounters. After a significant number of failed spiritual attempts, Satan changed tactics and began influencing people in this world against me.

The initial attack involved the theft of my business inventory, effectively decimating my entire business. A prostitute somehow accessed the hair extension inventory and stole it all. Until then, I had never fallen victim to a crime. Following this, I fell prey to a deceitful vehicle purchase, resulting in a huge financial loss. Such occurrences had never happened to me before. Subsequently, I withdrew $1,000 in cash from a bank teller. Roughly an hour later, I received frantic calls—it turned out the teller had given me $2,500 and was on the verge of losing his job. This, too, was an attack from Satan. A tactic of stealing from me and then providing me with compensation. "You deserve it," "You've been wronged; take this chance to make up for it." Satan attempts to twist one's moral compass to compromise God's principles. I promptly returned the surplus funds to an ever-grateful bank teller.

After enduring successive spiritual attacks, witnessing my business crumble, and withstanding bribery attempts, none of which compromised my faith in God, Satan had only one course of action left; to erase me from the face of the earth.

Marked for Death:
In the Crosshairs of Darkness

It was a picturesque Saturday evening in October, and the sun was gently dipping below the horizon as we wrapped up a meeting with a contractor. The vision I cherished deeply was to establish a sanctuary, a refuge where orphans from all corners could discover peace, reconnect with nature, and break free from their difficulties. It was a dream of providing them with an opportunity for pure beauty and happiness, an experience unlike any they had ever known before.

My close friend Nelly and I had embarked on this journey by establishing a nonprofit foundation a year earlier, dedicated to assisting orphanages. Using my personal savings, I had recently acquired three acres of land nestled by a serene lake in the mountains. The property was a captivating stretch of land graced by majestic pine trees and featuring an expansive 330 feet of lakefront. Not a single neighboring house was in sight, as this piece of land was enveloped by thousands of acres of serene wilderness.

While the path to acquiring and completing the purchase of this land hadn't been without its challenges, the realization of our dream was finally tangible. We hoped to extend an invitation to orphanages from across the nation, granting them free access to this retreat, a place to camp, fish, barbecue, gather around campfires, and exchange stories. I had forged my fondest memories during camping trips with loved ones, and I desired to give this same opportunity to orphaned children.

As our meeting with the contractor concluded around 6:45pm on that beautiful evening, we embarked on the drive back. The journey stretched ahead, promising a roughly two-hour passage through the majestic mountains. I always savored this drive, relishing in the scenic beauty and the tranquility it offered. It was a precious time for me to unwind and contemplate the subsequent steps in materializing the dream of offering this haven to the children.

During our return drive, Nelly and I shared thoughts on the serenity and peace of the mountainous landscapes. About half an hour into our drive back, darkness descended, and that's when we encountered an unexpected sight. A pickup truck had come to a halt in the oncoming lane, its high beams glaring intensely, obscuring our view. While the situation was slightly odd, it didn't immediately raise alarm bells; vehicles halting on the road were commonplace in the area.

Vehicles had gathered behind the lead one, triggering my initial assumption that the vehicle had encountered mechanical issues on the ascent up the hill, inadvertently obstructing the others. Through the darkness, faint silhouettes emerged, as the headlights of the trailing cars illuminated them. "Something seems wrong," I remarked to Nelly. I slowed down as we neared the stopped vehicle. As my own headlights progressively illuminated the figures, a chilling revelation unfolded.

With my headlights gradually revealing their forms from their feet upwards, a disturbing sight became clear: they were aiming rifles directly at us. The unsettling realization deepened as the beams unveiled their upper-torso regions, confirming that these individuals were wearing ski masks. My car came to a halt approximately 20 yards in front of the masked gunmen.

In an instant, a flash materialized from the darkness, swiftly followed by the distinct sound that is all too familiar - a muzzle flash and the subsequent report of a gunshot interrupted the calm evening. In that flash of a second, the tranquility that had enveloped me moments earlier was mercilessly snatched away, a theft perpetrated by an invisible, intangible thief. It was as if the most priceless possession we cling to had been stolen from us: peace. The coming seconds and inches would prove pivotal, determining the fates of both Nelly and myself as the events that followed unfolded.

I swiftly shifted the car into reverse as the sound of gunshots reverberated around us. Darkness enveloped the vehicle, obscuring my view through the tinted windows. Instinctively, I maneuvered in reverse, aiming to distance us from the assailants. Any direction away from danger seemed better than where we were. I managed to navigate the vehicle around a corner, barely out of the gunmen's sight. Rolling down my window to gain better visibility, I focused on the back tires as I started a three-point turn to head back the way we came from.

However, as I shifted into drive, another truck laden with armed men swiftly caught up to us, discharging rounds in our direction. Desperation took hold as I realized our dire situation. Why was this happening!? Faced with the prospect of certain death if we remained in one spot while making the 3-point turn, I made the harrowing decision to accelerate headlong towards the roadblock and waiting gunmen. As we accelerated at full speed, rapid gunfire echoed through the night air as bullets penetrated the vehicle. Glass shattered, and the sound of thuds and impacts accompanied the barrage of bullets. A bullet came through the windshield, perilously close to Nelly's head, as another punctured the windshield between the two of us, the projectiles narrowly missing us both.

Navigating through the relentless barrage of gunfire, we surged past the roadblock. However, ensuing chaos brought forth another problem, an impending collision with a small truck that heard the gunfire and started to turn around, obstructing our path. The impact was jarring, launching us airborne before the vehicle rolled, eventually landing on its wheels. With urgency, I shouted to Nelly, "Get out and run into the woods!" Aware that the gunmen would converge within moments to end our lives.

Reaching the tree line, I swiftly dove under a barbed wire fence. I stopped and lifted the bottom wire for Nelly to pass beneath, but when I looked back, she wasn't there. My heart sank, but relief washed over me as she materialized in front of the headlights of the wrecked vehicle. "Nelly!" I cried out. She sprinted towards me and quickly dove under the barbed wire.

With the deafening echoes of gunshots as our backdrop, we plunged into the dense forest while being shot at. We ran with every-thing in us as an unrelenting barrage of sticks and thorns cut and stabbed us. Racing through the darkness, every fiber of our beings focused on escape. Finally, we discovered a concealed enclave deep within the woods, a momentary respite from the imminent danger. Astonishingly, Nelly had her cell phone, and there was service in the mountains. We were able to contact the police. Their response was measured, causing the formation of a protective force before rescuing us.

For over an hour, we remained concealed, uncertain whether our pursuers were closing in. Amid the shadows, uncertainty loomed, our breaths held in anticipation. Finally, we emerged from our hid-ing place, heartened by the sight of the police who had come to our aid. The outcome was nothing short of miraculous; despite the hail of bullets and the vehicular collision, we had emerged relatively unscathed.

While the detectives were inspecting the vehicle at the police station, they suddenly shouted and moved away from it in fear. I asked what was happening, and they informed me that there was a poisonous snake in the vehicle. This vehicle had been sitting upright on the roadway since the collision, so it was extremely difficult to under-stand how there would be a snake in it. Satan would later brag to me it was his "calling card." A message to me he had been there.

In the days that followed the attack, I was in complete shock at having lived through something so violent. Then I questioned God. "Why?

All I do is help orphans and assist people in healing. Why wouldn't I be the one person who You would protect? Why was I allowed to be a target? I work for you, God"! The spiritual side of the attempted murder was revealed to me about a week after the attack.

Revelations of the Spirit:
Beyond the Physical

A profound wave of hatred and anger surged through me about a week after the attack while I was lying down. Words spilled from my lips, a vile torrent: "Let's get messed up, let's inflict pain, let's dominate". I saw cocaine, drunkenness, debauchery. I was witnessing the attack unfold from the demons' perspective. The next scene revealed them on the road, full of hate and a thirst for dominance. They relished in spreading terror, delighting in the fear they sowed. Laughter echoed as they reveled in the fear of those approaching the roadblock. Amid the chaos, one voice exclaimed, "What is this?!" Another spat, "Who does this guy think he is?" I realized this was when I arrived at the roadblock. They were incensed by my absence of fear, fuming at my defiance of them. The demons derived pleasure from instilling terror. They said to each other, 'Let's give this guy something to be afraid of... pull the trigger! Pull the trigger!' They shouted, and I felt them influencing decisions. Dark, hateful decisions.

As the gunmen fired, a chorus of evil laughter erupted. Their arrogance surged, a triumphant darkness that proclaimed, "See what we've done, you fool!? Witness who holds dominion over this land!" I felt their complete and utter satisfaction in the terror they promoted. Yet, a shift in their attitude immediately set in; panic gripped them. Their communication, once hateful, now bore confusion and anxiety. "What? What?" they stammered among themselves; their voices tinged with panic. And then, in a frenzied desperation, a chilling revelation pierced through: "God is coming!!!" Panic reigned as they grappled with what was happening. "He never comes here! What's happening?" they cried out. Reality set in, God was coming to my aid. In their terror, they shrieked, "This is God's chosen one! Protect him! Do not let these fools harm him! Make them miss!" Then, in an instant, I was transported to a different perspective.

Through the Eyes of the Divine

I hovered above the treeline, gazing down at the roof of my vehicle as it raced toward the roadblock amidst a barrage of gunfire. Suddenly, I flew down from above the treeline into the interior of the vehicle in microseconds, instantly. A radiant white, pure light flooded the vehicle, emanating from every window to the outside. A profound sense of tranquility washed over me, accompanied by a calming presence more powerful than any peace I had experienced before. God was now revealing His act of love and protection over me.

Within this serene moment, a deliberate and unhurried interaction ensued. "Son, duck down here," He calmly spoke, and I promptly complied by ducking down. I would come to realize that precisely at that instant, I was passing through the heaviest gunfire, and a bullet had entered through the driver's side window, piercing at the chest-level of the driver's seat. Had I been sitting slightly more upright, the bullet would have struck me mid-chest.

In the same soothing tone, God informed me of an impending collision. *"There's a collision approaching, son. Sit up straight, so the impact won't harm you."* I calmly adjusted my posture, just a split second before the impact. With a serene command, God guided the vehicle to land on its wheels, ensuring we could easily open the doors and make our escape.

"Son, inform Nelly that she needs to exit the vehicle and run for the woods." Me relaying the command instantly. Acting on His guidance, I swiftly crawled under the fence and paused. *"Son, Nelly can't see you.*

30

Call out to her. "At that moment, I saw her in front of the headlights, looking for me. As she caught up with me and we dashed into the woods, I witnessed God's extraordinary pure bright presence enveloping us, a protective shield ensuring our safety.

In the Blink of an Eye:
Immediate Judgement

God then showed me an investigative trial that unfolded immediately after the attempted murder. I sensed the rage emanating from God—*Satan!* He bellowed, *"Appear before me now!"* Satan materialized, seemingly unfazed. "Yes, God?" he retorted. *"I ordered you to stay away from my son! You have defied me!"* Satan feigned innocence, saying, "I have no knowledge of it, God. They acted on their own."

Without delay, God summoned the demons involved in the attack, demanding a reckoning from them. Trembling with fear, they stood before God. *"Why did you attack my son?"* He demanded; his tone forceful. The demons stumbled over their words, claiming ignorance of my "chosen" status. "We didn't know he was your chosen one, God", they stammered. Disgusted, God asked, *"How many others have passed through that area without fear present in them?"* Reluctantly, the demons confessed, "None." God's disdain was unmistakable. *"You are fools and an affront to me. For your crimes against Creation, you will be judged immediately."* God swiftly judged them for their role in the attack.

"Satan!" God thundered, still sensing His wrath over the defiance of His command to leave me alone. *"Bring me General Abadar!"* God demanded. Satan pleaded, "Please, God, spare him. I regret what happened, but this is too much." *"Present General Abadar before me now,"* God commanded. I comprehended that General Abadar was a close confidant and a long-serving associate of Satan. Satan held

unshakeable trust in him. It became apparent that General Abadar was in charge of orchestrating violence within the Creation.

"Who sanctioned the attack on my son?" God inquired of General Abadar. "Satan did," he admitted." *"Are you unaware that he has been chosen by me?"* God pressed. "Yes, I am aware, God. But I was acting under orders," General Abadar replied. I discerned that the allegiance of the general to Satan made him a prized asset, capable of defying God's command if Satan wanted him to.

God continued his line of questioning. *"How did you facilitate the assault on my son?"* The general named Jose, Rodrigo, Juan, and Diego as people under their influence in the area. "We had our soldiers influence them to take your son's life," he confessed. God, having heard enough, said *"For your crimes against the Creation, you shall be judged now,"* passing judgment on General Abadar.

"Satan!" God's voice resonated forcefully; the lingering anger evident in Him. *"Provide me with a captain for immediate judgment."* Once more, Satan pleaded, "God, please, no more. You have done enough. I understand, and it will not happen again." Firmly, God commanded, *"Present me with one of your captains for judgment."* Satan complied, and God promptly judged the captain for his crimes against Creation.

"Satan! Give me a lieutenant for judgment," God commanded. Satan's pleas intensified; "No, please, don't do this! General Abadar's judgment was overwhelming, and now you demand more?" Unyielding, God demanded, *"Provide me a lieutenant now, Satan."* The lieutenant was presented and swiftly judged for his crimes against the Creation.

"I want 30 demons before me," God decreed. At this, I witnessed Satan casting himself before God, imploring, "Mercy, mercy, mercy, mercy, God!" He beseeched God for mercy, his desperation clear. God's wrath receded. A sense of calm and tranquility descended. In a commanding voice, God declared, *"If a single hair on his head is harmed by*

your hand, I shall certainly judge you for it. You do not decide who lives and who dies. This is My Creation! Do not test me, Satan."

Below are the photos of the vehicle following Satan's attack:

Vehicle day after attack

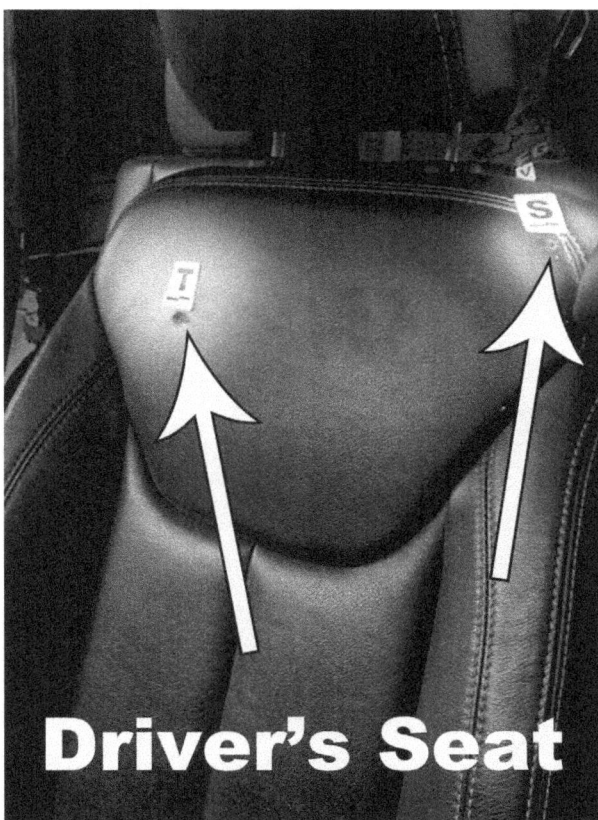

Driver's Seat

The True Cost of Serving God

I had always yearned to serve God, from the innocence of childhood when I sought God's presence in my life at just five years old, to the man who narrowly escaped paying the ultimate price. Somewhere between those two points, I strayed down my own path a time or two, but God never forgot about the sensitive heart of that little boy. But what is the cost of serving God? God's own son, who came to deliver a message of hope to us all and shoulder a debt that wasn't his, had only three years in ministry before being slain for sharing God's love with the world. How could pure love be destroyed so quickly on this earth?

What about the disciples? James was the first disciple to be martyred after Jesus. There are rumors they crucified Peter upside down, as he felt unworthy of dying in the same manner as Jesus. And the apostle Paul? While historical records may debate the exact date and method of Paul's death, it's widely accepted that he was also a martyr. Based on the events of that era, Paul likely met his end through beheading, possibly around the same time as Peter's crucifixion. The list goes on and on.

Why would men who spread love, God's light, be met with violence? Even God's own son? Isn't that fate reserved for criminals? Thieves? Mafia? Narcos? The underworld? Why would those who serve God be destined for such a grim outcome? Yes, those were different times. Have things evolved? We live in a more cultured era now, don't we? We inhabit educated societies with well-defined laws and modern enforcement mechanisms. There are police, courts, and penitentiaries. It's against the law to take a life, isn't it? This is what I had believed.

When I embarked on the journey of delivering messages of hope for God and removing demons, I became a major threat to Satan. I unknowingly became marked for death. The sole reason I stand here today is because of God. Clearly, God has a distinct plan for me, one that doesn't culminate in an untimely death for serving Him.

I have done and been many things in this life. I've been a Sheriff's Deputy, a Motorcycle Officer, a SWAT team member, endured 2 ½ years in Iraq during the peak of the conflict, and embarked on a solo motorcycle journey from the Canadian border to Colombia, South America. Dangerous professions and adventures by any measure. But what's the most dangerous job and adventure of my life? That's an easy one, serving God.

Now that my story has been told, we will embark on a journey deep into the spiritual world of the unseen. These revelations were the reason Satan tried to kill me. The truth is feared by the one that promotes lies and deceit to contaminate God's people. The journey that follows in these pages will be deep and unmask lies you have believed your whole life. Truths contained within these pages will be revealed to the ones with open hearts to see the truth. God bless you as you continue down this path of understanding that ultimately leads to a life-altering decision. Where will you spend eternity?

Psychedelics Unmasked: The Gateway

Becoming increasingly popular again for their emotional and mental healing properties, but are they truly the gateway drug, as the majority are led to believe? For the purpose of this conversation, we will discuss mushrooms, commonly known as magic mushrooms. These are all-natural, earthly creations of God. While there are other psychedelics with similar properties, our focus will be on exploring the moral implications of perceiving the truth through what God has created: psychedelic mushrooms.

Individuals who identify as God-fearing conservative Christians often uphold strict adherence to rules and laws. The government, however, deemed mushrooms illegal and used propaganda to instill the idea that trying them would lead to brain damage, thus labeling them as evil. This kind of manipulation is unsettling. To those individuals, I offer a single word: abortion. The very same government legalized it and deemed it good, a woman's right to terminate an unborn child. Could the same darkness responsible for endorsing the termination of innocent lives also be concealing truths from you? Is it plausible that this same force criminalized a natural plant that reveals the truth within us? Ponder this deeply, for it presents a profound moral dilemma for many.

On the opposite end of the spectrum, there are those who champion personal freedom, hold anti-government sentiments, and embody a hippie ethos. Have they discovered truths that others are hesitant to acknowledge? My intention here is not to pass judgment on differing viewpoints, but to uncover the truth. The truth about mushrooms, their existence on Earth, and the revelations they offer. To offer the truth and guidance about making choices while influenced by their effects.

In this revelation, we aim to shed light on the mysterious nature of mushrooms, their purpose in our world, and the profound insights they can provide. Let us uncover the layers of darkness and embrace the profound questions they present.

Allow me to establish my authority on this subject by revealing the extensive number of sessions in which I've been involved. First, these are referred to as "sessions" because they provide a dedicated period for healing, isolated from the external world. In my context, a session entails an individual reclining on a bed, their eyes covered, and meditative music softly playing in the background. Throughout most of the session, we leave them undisturbed in the room, enabling them to turn their focus inward. When they are awake, with eyes open or engaged in conversation, they direct their attention outward.

However, it is crucial to emphasize that genuine healing originates from within. I am resolute in my belief that individuals must delve into their inner selves to uncover answers during a session. This is a powerful form of medicine that demands respect. I firmly reject the notion that recreational psychedelics taken with other people possess the capability for substantial healing, primarily because of external distractions.

As of the time of writing, I have been involved with 432 psychedelic sessions for individuals beyond the borders of the United States. Being sensitive to the spirit grants a distinct advantage when guiding these sessions. It allows me to perceive the inner workings of a person. Yet, it can also be a double-edged sword. During my initial season on this path of aiding people in overcoming their inner turmoil, I failed to realize the impact it was having on me. I grew exceedingly irritated with the people doing their sessions and desired to distance myself from them. I temporarily suspended my role as a guide because the emotional toll became overwhelming.

When a person is in a session, their vulnerability and openness are heightened. This heightened state enables them to observe and release their internal struggles. Something intimately connected me with the darkness that was brought to the surface, and the experience was emotionally grueling for me. Over time, I gradually learned how to shield myself from this overwhelming influence, allowing me to resume my mission of facilitating healing for others.

I once watched a YouTuber discuss her first psychedelic experience. She ingested a substantial amount of mushrooms and wandered around her house, eventually venturing outside into the street. The woman appeared to be a Christian, attempting to fulfill God's work by warning people about the dangerous effects of these psychedelics. She detailed her encounter with intense darkness, which she identified as demons, actively pursuing her. They convinced this person that the experience had opened a gateway to Satan, and she passionately advocated for complete avoidance of these substances. Her intentions were undoubtedly good; she genuinely believed in her cause. However, what she witnessed was introspective. She came face-to-face with the internal demons she carried, which deeply frightened her. In the end, she saw the truth. She just didn't know how to interpret it or what it meant.

The Devil's Gateway?

I, too, had undergone transformative healing through the use of mushrooms. I knew that, under the right conditions, they could yield incredibly positive healing. Still, a nagging question lingered: why did these substances even exist on Earth? For a considerable stretch of time, I grappled with this inquiry alone. I observed both their positive and negative impacts on different people, witnessing individuals engaging in one or two sessions and then retreating hastily, while a small minority persevered beyond seven or eight sessions, unswervingly pursuing truth. In Matthew 7:7-8, it says: *"Ask, and it will be given to you; seek, and you will find; knock, and the door will be opened to you. For everyone who asks receives; the one who seeks finds; and to the one who knocks, the door will be opened."* But can this biblical verse apply to the use of mushrooms?

The answer to my quest for truth was eventually unveiled to me by God one evening. He transported me to the Garden of Eden, revealing Adam and Eve standing before the Tree of Knowledge of Good and Evil. God emphasized His desire to never withhold truth from His children, granting them the freedom to choose. The tree existed so that they could choose the knowledge of good and evil if they so desired. In a similar manner, God has provided us with mushrooms. These fungi serve as a gateway to truth, the understanding of good and evil. The decision to embrace this knowledge is left to His children.

Satan does not want you to see the darkness within. His demons find refuge there, using it as their base of operation. This is the principal reason most governments have criminalized the consumption of this natural substance. Make no mistake, Satan wields considerable influence within the Creation.

Four Paths, One Revelation:
Journeying to the Truth

I have observed people emerging from these sessions with fresh ideas, labeling them as spiritual guidance. I, too, have left sessions with new job concepts, business plans, and revelations that I hadn't experienced before. Convinced that these are messages from God, individuals often swiftly act upon them. Yet, I've encountered plans that appeared brilliant in the session but crumbled when put into action. So, was it truly the guiding hand of God? In some cases, it seems unlikely.

I believe psychedelics can potentially open previously unexplored neural pathways, giving rise to new thought patterns. Perhaps they render you slightly more creative than before the session. While the scientific understanding is still incomplete, I advise caution when labeling something from a session as divine. In my experience, ideas of this nature often surface towards the end of the session as the effects are subsiding, which would facilitate the new thought pattern theory.

On the path of psychedelic healing, I've had the opportunity to observe the emergence of only four distinct paths across hundreds of sessions. It's of utmost importance to grasp the concept that we are spiritual entities living within temporary physical bodies, destined to move on to another existence once our current one draws to a close. Disregarding the spiritual dimension is akin to turning away from the truth, limiting the opportunity for genuine healing through this process.

First Path: The initial path I have observed involves individuals engaging in around 1-3 sessions. They embark on a surface-level journey of cleansing and healing. Quick to claim triumph through these sessions, they exclaim, "I'm good, I feel fantastic, never been better." Undoubtedly, they are in the best state they've ever been, rating themselves at 9 out of a scale of 1-10, a level they deemed more than satisfactory to avoid further sessions. "Why risk it?" comes a deep thought from within themselves. But what exactly is the risk of continuing on the path to healing? Why gamble with uncovering the truth behind their pain? Why confront a reality they fear? Content with their progress, they vanish, never to return.

When confronted by someone asserting they are "good" and no longer need healing, I pose a question: "Good compared to what"? What is your yardstick for measuring well-being? How do you determine your standard of "good" in this life? To challenge their consciousness, I employ a slide rule technique. I depict a scale from 1 to 100, where 1 symbolizes being beaten down, carrying scars of sexual abuse, rejection, abandonment, physical and emotional abuse, neglect, and more. On the other end, 100 signifies perfection, radiating an incredible light as you walk this path of life. You are pure love with no programs to heal or pain to remove. Then I tell you to imagine you were at a mere 6 when you started to heal. After two sessions, you've ascended to 10, feeling the best you ever have. You've never felt so light and free as you do right now.

Convinced that you're "healed," how do you assess your position on the healing scale? Against what benchmark are you measuring your state of "good"? How do you know you were at a 6 and are now at a 10? This is where introspection comes into play, revealing the answers within you. These people declare victory out of fear of seeing the truth. Now, let's proceed to the second path that has developed within the healing circles.

Second Path: This road is intricate. The healing spans approximately 3-8 sessions, followed by a conclusion. These individuals delve into the abyss of rejection, confronting their past abuses and working through the pain. They address childhood traumas, making significant progress. Operating within the realm of the flesh, they tackle the psychological aftermath of their trauma and emerge relatively improved. However, their journey takes a spiritual twist when they encounter a formidable barrier.

Delving deeper, they collide with a spiritual impasse. Their resistance to embracing God enables Satan to obstruct genuine, profound healing. He thrives on their darkness, ensuring it remains intact. Fear is a very effective tool to prevent removing the deepest-rooted darkness. Without the authority to expel Satan's presence because of their refusal to acknowledge God, they remain stuck. They will often claim some form of triumph through their experiences with mushrooms, although their enthusiasm might not be as pronounced. Deep inside, they harbor an awareness that something significant was encountered. They caught a glimpse of it, but uncertainty lingered about how to navigate it, leading them to opt for leaving it untouched and carrying on with life.

I have witnessed instances where God permits individuals to rid themselves of certain demons, even before accepting Him into their lives. His boundless love allows this, enabling them to glimpse spiritual truth. This occurs for a select few, usually they can remove the demons exerting the strongest influence on the surface. Consider the example of the demon of hate, an evil and oppressive force. Removing hate creates space for love to emanate, contingent upon the individual's choice, of course. However, make no mistake, should they neglect to welcome God, the demon of hate will swiftly return.

Mathew 12:43-45 says: *"When an evil spirit leaves a person, it goes into the desert, seeking rest but finding none. Then it says, 'I will return to the person I came from.' So it returns and finds its former home empty, swept, and in order. Then the spirit finds seven other spirits more evil than itself, and they all enter the person and live there. And so that person is worse off than before. That will be the experience of this evil generation.*

The Bible is clear on this: you may remove the demon, but God needs to fill the void left behind. Without His presence, darkness can return and influence you even more. Next, we'll look at the third path that some travel down.

Third Path: This is the "enlightened" path, where you will find spiritual individuals walking. They connect with nature, feel the energy of life force around them, and advocate for love and unity among all. It's a path that Satan leads people down, a subtle diversion from the path to truth. Almost all empaths, and those sensitive to the spirit, fall for this deception. Loving others and connecting with the beauty of nature are commendable notions, right? Certainly. However, Satan's most significant deception on this road involves disguising demons as angels. Yes, you read that correctly. They exploit the very name of the beings that dwell with God as a powerful tool to ensnare unsuspecting people.

"But that can't be right," you might argue, thinking this truth has gone too far. Love, unity, connectivity and spirituality are all-inclusive, right? Let's turn to the Bible for a moment to reinforce this truth. In 2 Corinthians 11:14, Paul speaks of false prophets and states, *"Even Satan disguises himself as an angel of light."* How does this occur? After witnessing it from the spiritual side, I will reveal the truth behind this deception. Every one of us carries a fragment of God within us. We are all created from Him, and since God is light, we inherently possess that divine light. As we peel away layer after layer of darkness through healing, this inner light radiates more brilliantly within us.

Take your cell phone and activate the flashlight. Yes, right now, please. With the light shining away from you, place your hand about 3-4 inches in front of the light. Notice how the light reflects off your hand, intensifying its brightness? Is your hand the source of that brilliant light? Certainly not; it's merely reflecting light from the actual source. For empaths and those on a spiritual journey, this is how Satan appears as an angel of light to us. It is a mere reflection off of him, we perceive as illumination. This deception is profoundly cunning.

I cannot count the endless deceptions I've encountered on this journey. Satan and his legion are unrelenting in their trickery. They have duped and misled everyone I know countless times. One time, I was assisting a friend in removing some demons, a physically exhausting endeavor. She could not release, so I had to do most of the work. After about 40 minutes of work, I heard a voice say, "Son, you have worked diligently today. Both of you deserve rest. Thank you for your tireless efforts". I thought to myself, "Sure, I'm exhausted, and if God wants me to rest, then I'll rest. After all, we've made significant progress so far"! I promptly discovered that this was a deceit designed to prevent me from removing any more darkness.

In the beginning of this path, God had taught me how to test the voices I heard. How to discern His voice above all the other noise. Over time, you become familiar with God's voice. However, in the beginning, when you hear in the spirit, it is the faintest of whispers, distinguishing what you hear is challenging. Demons are masterful deceivers; they won't command you to offer your firstborn child as a sacrifice to them on an altar. Instead, they entice with a subtle detour that may sound appealing but slowly leads you away from God. Why would the witch from earlier suggest lighting candles to Catholic saints? Are you focusing on God, or are you being led astray by the slight diversion of idolizing deceased people who walked the Earth?

To whom do you pray? Do you pray to another deceased human? What? No! That's utter nonsense! What about Mary, the mother of Jesus? What about the saints? These are just slight deviations from God's path. What about mother nature? Do you attempt to connect with the creation rather than the Creator? Focusing on trees and plants more than the One who fashioned them? These are minor detours, yet enough to distance you from eternity with God.

It's reminiscent of target practicing with a bow and arrow. From the moment the arrow leaves the guide of the bow, the trajectory of the flight path is directed by where the sights were aimed at that moment. If the sights are 1/8 of an inch off the bullseye when the arrow is launched, the trajectory of the arrow can miss the entire target. That's all Satan has to do. Take your sights off God just a tiny bit, and he has you off target when you breathe your last breath.

A deception found on this path is "there is no good or bad". Once Satan convinces them that everything is love and beauty, they stop looking for the darkness within. This creates a safe haven for Satan to operate from, with no fear of being discovered.

People who follow the third path will never find the truth about the darkness. If they can't find it, they can't remove it. The darkness will pivot, move, and change places within the body, but the true, deep-down darkness, the source, will never leave. Those on this path accept the belief that 'no one can ever really be healed. Healing is a path you will be on until death.' It's a lie deeply ingrained within them, causing them to delve into more healing rituals and deception. Satan will give them momentary respite from their pain and trauma, and some superficial healing will keep them believing the lie. But salvation will elude them, and Satan will always ensure it's just out of reach.

Next, let's delve into the fourth and final path that plays a crucial role in the psychedelic healing process.

Fourth Path: Within our group of people healing, we have 91 individuals who have successfully completed 432 sessions. An astounding 96% of them have fallen into the first three paths. Only 4% have followed this fourth path of healing. It is undoubtedly the most challenging and demanding journey to undertake. The level of attacks, lies and deception is mind-boggling. It was on this fourth path that I was robbed, cheated, and almost lost my life. Why is this path so perilous? Because this is where the lie is unearthed.

This path leads to the truth. Is the truth all about rainbows, unicorns, sunshine, and flowers? No, that's the deception. The real truth is that Satan has thoroughly contaminated the creation. His darkness pervades everywhere. Once you become conscious of this darkness within, you become a significant threat to Satan. But why does only a small percentage make it to the fourth path? Because you, on your own, cannot reach this path. Yes, that is correct. You cannot accomplish it.

Your strength is insufficient to pierce the darkness and illuminate the truth. Only God possesses the might and power to reveal the depths of darkness. Satan is exceedingly intelligent, sly, and deceitful. Even approaching his darkness to remove it is beyond your capacity. He has perfected his skills in deception over thousands of years. He has killed countless prophets, disciples, and even God's own son for daring to unveil the truth. And what about you? Whether you've been on this healing journey for 1, 2, 5, or even 10 years matters little. Even if you've dedicated 50 years to this path, you are no match for Satan's mastery of deceit.

What if I don't believe in God or have no desire to? In that case, Satan has already triumphed. He has persuaded you to embrace a massive lie that will cost you dearly. Such is his ability to contaminate the creation and lead God's children away from Him. At best, you will remain on the third path, only to confront the truth upon death, when it's too late for you.

Through psychedelics, one can only find the truth on one path. You can heal some pain and relieve some anxiety through the three other paths. Only with an open heart towards God will you know which path you are on. These are the indicators of each path, but the heart reveals all that is within a man. So ask yourself this very important question: Where is my heart on this journey?

After writing about the fourth path, I went to bed. During the night, I had a vision, and God told me to proclaim what I had seen to the world. So, I am here writing this down first thing in the morning while everything is still fresh. This, is that vision:

The Vision

Vision: I found myself deep inside a prison. I heard banging sounds and tried to locate their source. After a few attempts, I peered through a small hole. Three individuals were there, wielding a hammer and chisel, relentlessly striking the center of the structure. Eventually, a larger-than-expected chunk of the structure broke away and crashed just a few feet below. From the point of impact, I noticed small hair-line cracks spreading outward. The damage they had caused was catastrophic for the prison's integrity.

Filled with panic, I rushed around, trying to find my friends to warn them about the impending collapse. I reached a gate that was padlocked. Some of my friends were visible, dressed in guard uniforms. I shouted their names, but only one responded. She approached the gate, and I urgently yelled to everyone I could, "The structure is collapsing; we must leave now!" She opened the gate, and we entered the structure to escape from the back.

Navigating through debris and obstacles, we fled through the back as others tried to escape as well. The collapsing structure caught some, while others mistakenly believed they were safe within it. I watched as they were left behind while we exited the building. Once in a field behind the prison, many people halted, thinking they were now out of danger.

I urged my friend, "No, we must keep going." We ran to the edge of a forest, where only a few others were present. Looking back at the prison, we witnessed thousands of people who had climbed onto the roof screaming for help. As the building collapsed, it disappeared from view, taking thousands with it. My friend turned to me and said, "Thank you for saving me." I replied, "You were saved because of your heart."

Suddenly, as we concluded our conversation, a landslide began. The prison was crumbling into a massive hole that was swallowing the surrounding land. All those who had paused in the field, believing they were safe, were swept away. The ground beneath us gave way, and we were drawn toward the hole. Despite the surrounding chaos, there was a profound sense that God was shielding us from the destruction, even though we were affected by it.

As the gaping hole filled with earth, we came to a stop. We were waist-deep in dirt and debris, yet somehow safe. Amidst taking in the scene, I detected a strong sewer-like smell in the surrounding air.

That was the vision. In the morning, I asked God for the interpretation, as he has done so many times with messages for people.

Interpretation: The prison serves as a symbol for the earth itself. The figures tirelessly chipping away at the core, aiming to dismantle it, are demons, agents of Satan working relentlessly towards the destruction of the earth. In a spiritual state, God granted me a glimpse through the cracks, witnessing their actions. He revealed their actions to me, compelling me to urgently warn anyone I could reach.

The locked prison doors signify the confines of the flesh. I found myself trapped by the limitations of the physical world, unable to break free. I called out to my friends, and only one could hear my pleas. The guard uniforms they wore represent authority, the inherent power each person possesses to determine their path on this earth. Their individual authority, grounded in free will, outweighed mine, which is why they didn't care about my warning.

Escaping the prison amidst debris and collapsing structures represents an impending destruction that will fall upon the earth. People who run but halt prematurely symbolize those who won't inherit God's kingdom. To claim that inheritance, one must persist to the very end without faltering. Some may run farther than others and use that as a measure of their goodness. However, they, too, will be swept away, as God never truly recognized them. They never reached Him. These are the individuals who mistakenly believe that merely discussing God or performing good deeds suffices for His salvation.

Matthew 7:22-23 reads, "On judgment day many will say to me, 'Lord! Lord! We prophesied in your name and cast out demons in your name and performed many miracles in your name.' But I will reply, 'I never knew you. Get away from me, you who break God's laws.'"

The forest we reached symbolizes our arrival at the destination that God had planned for us. Salvation of my friend resulted from her righteous heart and her alignment with God's will. The ensuing landslide represents a second wave of destruction that will occur immediately afterward. Even though those firmly rooted in God will sense the earth trembling beneath their feet and feel the impact of the destruction, they will remain under His protective shield.

The foul smell at the end of the vision was the smell of death contaminating the air. The decaying lives that once were. At the end of the interpretation, God reassured me I will bear witness to this vision within my lifetime.

This vision is intended for those who will listen and heed its message. As the times become increasingly difficult, it is imperative that you remain steadfast in seeking God until the very end; otherwise, you may find yourself swept away by the turmoil of the world.

Empaths-Witches and Prophets

In a world where scientific understanding constantly evolves, one phenomenon that continues to captivate researchers and individuals alike is the mysterious nature of empaths. These unique individuals possess an extraordinary ability to innately and deeply sense the emotions and feelings of those around them. While science has made significant strides in deciphering the complexities of empathy, many aspects of this phenomenon remain shrouded in fascination.

Empaths, as they are more recently known, appear to have an innate sensitivity to the emotional states of others. They can often pick up on subtle cues in body language, facial expressions, tone of voice, and even energy patterns. This heightened awareness allows them to not only comprehend the emotions of people around them, but also experience those emotions as if they were their own.

At the core of empathic abilities lies the concept of mirror neurons, specialized brain cells that fire both when we perform a specific action and when we observe someone else performing the same action. These neurons create a bridge between self and others, enabling empaths to simulate in their minds the emotional experiences of those they interact with. It's as if their neural wiring blurs the lines between individual emotional boundaries, resulting in an almost seamless emotional resonance with others.

Recent research in neuroscience suggests that empaths might have unique patterns of brain activation and connectivity. Studies have revealed differences in brain regions associated with emotional processing, such as the anterior insula and the anterior cingulate cortex. These areas are thought to play a pivotal role in recognizing and experiencing emotions, providing a potential neural basis for empathic abilities.

However, the scientific journey into understanding empaths is far from conclusive. Questions linger about the precise genetic, neural, and environmental factors that contribute to someone becoming an empath. While some believe that genetic predisposition could influence the development of empathic traits, others speculate that early childhood and social upbringing might also play a significant role.

The experiences of empaths themselves provide valuable insights. Many report that their ability to feel others' emotions deeply can be both a blessing and a challenge. On one hand, it allows them to forge profound connections, offer unparalleled support, and navigate complex social dynamics with finesse. On the other hand, this intense emotional sensitivity can lead to emotional exhaustion, difficulty in distinguishing their own feelings from those of others, and a need for solitude to recharge.

In a world where understanding and empathy are prized, empaths serve as living reminders of the power of emotional connection. Their abilities can help bridge gaps in communication and foster a deeper understanding of diverse perspectives. In therapeutic settings, empaths can be incredibly effective at helping others process their emotions and find solace in times of distress.

As science continues its exploration of the human mind and emotions, the phenomenon of empaths remains a captivating area of study. While our understanding has undoubtedly grown, there is much yet to uncover about the intricacies of this unique ability. As researchers delve deeper into the neural science of empathy and its variations, the stories and experiences of empaths themselves will continue to shape our evolving understanding of what it truly means to connect with others on an emotional level. That is the world's understanding of an empath. Let's dive into the truth of what an empath really is.

Empaths: The Truth Unearthed

Empaths are individuals who possess a profound connection to their spirits. Understanding that we were created from the spiritual realm and will eventually return to it is crucial. Our physical bodies, mere temporary vessels, house our journey toward the spiritual destination we choose once our earthly existence is over. It's imperative to recognize that we are spiritual beings within bodies, not mere bodies with spirits.

An empath's unique trait lies in their heightened connection between their mind and spirit, far surpassing the norm. It is within the spiritual realm that all truths are revealed. Our spirits, in harmony with one another, intertwine and connect. According to scientists, we are energy. Speculation has arisen, suggesting that the energy emanating from others is what an empath perceives when in close proximity. This profound connection we share with others finds its roots within the spirit. Regrettably, most individuals remain out of touch with their spiritual selves. Bound by ego, ensnared by the mind and body, they see through physical eyes and hear through their physical ears. The hurried sensory perceptions of the body have eclipsed the sensitivity to the spirit. So people demand to hear "I love you" audibly, unable to perceive the love already connected through the spirit.

God has deliberately created a select group of people who connect with unparalleled sensitivity to their spirit. This particular creation grants God a voice in the creation's vastness if the people choose to hear His voice. These people are divinely equipped for direct communication with Him, becoming vessels for transmitting messages of hope and love. In biblical times, we knew them as prophets.

However, the question arises: what detours an empath destined to forge an extraordinary connection with God? The answer: Satan. From the onset, Satan identifies these individuals as prime targets, given their immense potential value. Satan also lives in the spiritual realm, with access to the entire creation. Recognizing that early intervention is vital, he seeks to ensnare empaths for his own dark purposes.

So how does he do this? The Prince of Darkness primarily targets empaths through their principal source of influence in their early years: their parents. God safeguards a child's salvation until consciousness, which typically occurs around the age of 12, from that point onward, they have to choose God for their salvation. Aware of this, Satan aims to infiltrate the empath's life as early as possible, knowing their parents remain vulnerable to his influence. Through various means, such as rejection, abandonment, physical violence, emotional degradation, sexual abuse, and humiliation, Satan generates profound and intense pain within the child, a darkness potent enough for him to occupy when the child reaches consciousness.

In my life, my father was extremely abusive towards me. Among my four siblings, I was the sole recipient of continuous beatings, ridicule, and emotional abuse. This inflicted pain fostered a deep-seated hatred within me. I harbored resentment towards my abusive father and my mother, who failed to protect me from his abuse. However, I've released this darkness by forgiving them both. Over time, I comprehended the reasons behind the harsh treatment I endured, unlike my siblings. The isolation and emotional abuse I faced were tools used by Satan to manipulate me. These experiences were orchestrated to pave the way for Satan's influence to take hold within me, exploiting me for a campaign of misinformation against God.

In the complex spiritual world beyond our understanding, a battle between light and darkness ensues. Empaths serve as conduits through which both God and Satan reach out. God to speak the truth of hope and love to His children and Satan to deceive and lie to the people that will listen. The empath's journey winds through the fabric of spirituality, navigating the battleground between positive and negative forces. Within their personal experiences, we discover the story of how empaths forge connections with the spiritual world, leaving a lasting impact on the ongoing struggles of this life.

Next, let's delve into how Satan employs empaths and those who are sensitive to the spirit to achieve his objective of complete destruction of the creation.

Unveiling the Secrets:
Spirituality-Witchcraft-Sorcery-Magic

I am feeling physically sick, and I'm almost at the point of throwing up as I delve into this darkness. However, I've committed to telling the truth, and the truth includes both sides of this spiritual war. If you've never ventured into this territory, feel free to skip past this part. Understand that intimate knowledge of the darkness isn't necessary at all in order for God to heal you.

In a world guided by reason and practical understanding, the concepts of witchcraft and spirituality have often found themselves at the crossroads of fascination and skepticism. Embedded in folklore and history, the term "witchcraft" has evolved over time, shaping perceptions and beliefs across cultures. From a scientific standpoint, witchcraft is a complex interweaving of psychology, social dynamics, spirituality, and cultural phenomena that have sparked curiosity and inquiry. But at its core, it's the harnessing of Satan's influence over the creation.

In the pages of the Bible, the concepts of sorcery and witchcraft are woven into the tapestry of ancient narratives, offering insights into how these practices were perceived within the cultural and religious context of the time. The Bible presents a mix of cautionary tales, historical events, and spiritual teachings that shed light on the interactions between God and the spiritual truth.

Throughout the Old Testament, instances of sorcery and witch-craft are depicted as practices that run counter to God's will and commandments. In Exodus 22:18, the command *"You shall not allow a sorceress to live"* emphasizes the serious nature of engaging in such practices. This perspective arises from the belief that sorcery and witchcraft involved seeking supernatural power through means other than God's connection, challenging the authority and sover-eignty of God.

The story of Saul and the witch of Endor in 1 Samuel 28 is a notable example of God's stance on witchcraft. Faced with impending battle and desperation, King Saul seeks a medium to conjure the spirit of the deceased prophet Samuel. The passage illustrates the forbidden nature of consulting with mediums and attempting to communicate with the dead. The narrative underscores the importance of relying on God for guidance and highlights the potential dangers of engag-ing in practices that bypass His authority.

In the New Testament, the spread of Christianity brought forth a shift in focus from ancient practices to the teachings of Christ. However, the story of Simon the Sorcerer in Acts 8 offers insight into how sorcery was perceived in the early Christian context. The miracles performed by the apostles intrigue Simon, a magician from Samaria, and seeks to purchase the power of the Holy Spirit. Peter's rebuke of Simon highlights the incompatibility of sorcery with the authentic work of God, emphasizing the importance of genuine faith and connection with God over spiritual manipulation.

While the Bible discourages sorcery and witchcraft, it also acknowl-edges the existence of spiritual forces beyond the material realm. The Bible's approach to these concepts serves to emphasize the suprem-acy of God's power and the importance of seeking a relationship with Him rather than relying on practices that attempt to conjure spiritual forces.

Exploring the Darkness:
Witches and Spiritual Guides

While they are distinct, they share the same purpose; to divert God's people away from Him. Spiritual Guides or Spiritual Influencers have become the new agents for Satan. They offer deception by channeling messages from their own ancestors or spiritual guides. Of course, by now, you know that these are demons pretending to be whatever being would be most alluring for people to connect with.

This is where approximately 98% of empaths find themselves. Once the pain has accumulated within their bodies, Satan positions his demons. A dark presence is now established, allowing them to start communication with the empath. Many empaths become confused, thinking they're hearing voices in their head or going crazy. Some even isolate themselves from society to escape the voices or to avoid connecting with others. Empaths are particularly susceptible to the influence of self-destructive thoughts, demons often manifesting as a dark voice, persuading them that life is not worthwhile, urging them to leave and forget this world. They push suicide as a viable escape from this world.

Then there are other empaths who embrace this road and the darkness it leads to. Their ego swells as they realize their capacity to tap into the supernatural. They gain insights about people, glimpse "future" events, and offer recommendations for healing. They draw people to them because of their seemingly supernatural knowledge.

These empaths become potent tools for Satan. They attract people with their special abilities and insights into the unseen. Through these empaths, Satan's campaign of misdirection gains significant momentum.

In contemplating this narrative, we encounter a sobering truth. The choices made by empaths hold the power to define their spiritual influence in this life. The narrative serves as a cautionary tale, urging us to discern the forces at play and recognize the importance of safeguarding our spiritual connection with God from the seductive call of Satan. In this convergence of paths, the battle between light and darkness continues to unfold, reminding us of the enduring struggle of God for our salvation.

Do you recall the witch we encountered earlier in this book? Extreme poverty and persistent troubles marked her life. Despite possessing a "special gift" for aiding people through her connection to the other side, her existence was full of distress. Ailments plagued her frequently, and her health deteriorated in her thirties. The threat of losing her job loomed over her perpetually.

She guided her husband in life decisions, her children began hearing voices from their own "spiritual guides," and she encouraged them to embrace these voices. On one occasion, her daughter faced ridicule at school, and in response, she cursed a person for it. While the precise repercussions evade my memory, I believe the target of the curse suffered a fall and broke their arm the following day. The witch took immense pride in her 12-year-old daughter's seemingly potent power.

How do such occurrences manifest? Is the power authentic? How do the demons convey specific information to this witch, such as the person from whom I would be robbed, which ultimately materializes? How did the witch gain insights into my past, which she couldn't have known through conventional means? Are they endowed with supernatural abilities? Can they foresee the future? These questions, among others, will find their answers in the following chapters.

1 Timothy 4:1: *"Now the Holy Spirit tells us clearly that in the last times some will turn away from the true faith; they will follow deceptive spirits and teachings that come from demons."*

Chakras: Unveiling the Deception and Seeking Truth

Chakras, originating from ancient Eastern spiritual traditions, are believed to exist within the human body. This concept is deeply rooted in practices like yoga and meditation. The term "chakra" is derived from the Sanskrit word for "wheel" or "disk," reflecting the swirling nature of these energy points and their role in maintaining a harmonious connection between the body, mind, and spirit.

According to the belief, there are seven main chakras positioned along the central axis of the body, running from the base of the spine to the crown of the head. Each chakra is associated with a specific color, vibration, and aspect of human experience, representing a unique sphere of influence on our well-being.

The belief in chakras emphasizes the flow of vital energy through these energy centers. When chakras are in balance and energy flows freely, it is thought to contribute to physical, emotional, and spiritual well-being. However, blockages or imbalances in these energy centers can cause various forms of discomfort, illness, or spiritual disharmony.

Practices such as meditation, yoga, and "energy healing" aim to cleanse and balance the chakras, fostering optimal energy flow throughout the body. Visualization, breathwork, and focused intention are often used to target specific chakras and address their associated aspects of life.

This is yet another enticing diversion from God that one is likely to encounter. All 'spiritual influencers' tend to recommend this as a means of connecting with oneself. One of the initial gifts given to me by the witch was a personalized coffee mug. It featured chakras on one side and my name on the other. According to her 'spiritual guide's' counsel, I was advised to focus more on my energy centers. Sounds like sound advice, doesn't it? Well, if you're Satan aiming to lead people away from communicating with a God who would offer salvation, then yes, it would indeed be considered fantastic guidance.

REMEMBER: ANYTHING, NO MATTER HOW SUBTLE, THAT DIVERTS YOUR ATTENTION FROM GOD, WILL BE USED AGAINST YOU. Questions regarding chakras typically evoke this response from me: *Only a witch and a demon have ever instructed me to follow their guidance on chakras, and I have NEVER come across any mention of chakras in the Bible.*

Unmasking Illusions: The deceit of no good or bad in the world

You'll encounter this perspective within the healing realms of spirituality: "There is no good, there is no bad. They are just abstracts of the mind designed to generate pain and suffering." It might strike you as profound, a concept worth embracing. After all, if there is no notion of bad, then perhaps I'm shielded from my suffering. We create all suffering from within, an illusion of the mind, according to this concept. I could simply adjust my mindset and disregard acts of murder, rape, child abuse, and all the other atrocities under the sun. On the other side of this, there is no concept of good either. If the concept of good can be eliminated from the mind, then there's no source of hope in the One who embodies goodness.

Yet, there's a deception artfully woven into this narrative, slipped into the very fabric of healing circles, and it serves to aid Satan's foothold within you. By discarding the existence of evil, it effectively discourages you from looking for it. Without you looking for it, there's no way for you to remove it. Satan then has a safe place to work from. We provide a platform for the spreading of his deceit. This perspective of "there's no good or bad" might seem freeing, but it hides a dark purpose that lets Satan keep a hold on you.

Servants of Darkness: Unveiling Satan's Demons

In the ancient land of Eden, the deceptive whisper of a serpent marked humanity's first encounter with spiritual darkness. From that moment, the contamination of darkness stretched across the pages of our history, introducing us to an army of evil known as demons. These beings, intricately woven into the fabric of the scriptures, have played a role both threatening and detrimental in the unfolding story of the creation.

It wasn't until the Gospel narratives that the stage was truly illuminated, revealing the power struggle between light and darkness, as embodied by Jesus' interactions with demons in the New Testament:

Matthew 9:32-33 *"When they left, a demon-possessed man who couldn't speak was brought to Jesus. So Jesus cast out the demon, and then the man began to speak. The crowds were amazed. "Nothing like this has ever happened in Israel!" they exclaimed"*.

Matthew 17:14-21 *"At the foot of the mountain, a large crowd was waiting for them. A man came and knelt before Jesus and said, "Lord, have mercy on my son. He has seizures and suffers terribly. He often falls into the fire or into the water. So I brought him to your disciples, but they couldn't heal him." Jesus said, "You faithless and corrupt people! How long must I be with you? How long must I put up with you? Bring the boy here to me." Then Jesus rebuked the demon in the boy, and it left him. From that moment the boy was well.*

19 Afterward the disciples asked Jesus privately, "Why couldn't we cast out that demon?"

"You don't have enough faith," Jesus told them. "I tell you the truth, if you had faith even as small as a mustard seed, you could say to this mountain, 'Move from here to there,' and it would move. Nothing would be impossible."

Along with Jesus' ministry in the gospels, there are several additional accounts of interactions with demons in the New Testament. These encounters highlight the ongoing spiritual battles and the authority of God over Satan's demons.

The New Testament illustrates that the conflict with demonic forces did not end with Jesus' ministry, but continues to this very day. The following verses from the New Testament confirm that the battle with demons persists in the lives of God's children:

1 Peter 5:8-9 *"Stay alert! Watch out for your great enemy, the devil. He prowls around like a roaring lion, looking for someone to devour. Stand firm against him, and be strong in your faith. Remember that your family of believers all over the world is going through the same kind of suffering you are."* This verse serves as a reminder that believers must remain vigilant against the schemes of the enemy, suggesting a continuous spiritual struggle.

Ephesians 6:12 *"For we are not fighting against flesh-and-blood enemies, but against evil rulers and authorities of the unseen world, against mighty powers in this dark world, and against evil spirits in the heavenly places."* This verse highlights the ongoing spiritual battle we face against dark forces.

In the region of Gadara, the Gospels of Matthew, Mark, and Luke recount a haunting tale. Two demon-possessed men, living among the tombs, met Jesus in a confrontation that shook the foundations of our reality. Jesus' words were a commanding summons, piercing the darkness that had ensnared these men. *"Come out of the man, you evil spirit!"* (Mark 5:8). With unparalleled authority, Jesus expelled the demons, casting them into a herd of about 2,000 pigs. The entire herd then plunged down the steep hillside into the lake and drowned in the water (Mark 5:13).

The encounter with Legion, as the demons identified themselves, showcased the realm of spiritual warfare. A struggle not confined to earthly battles, but fought within the very fabric of the spirit. Jesus's power over these evil forces showed that the ultimate authority rests with God.

Progressing in time, Paul's writings reveal further dimensions of demonology. In his letter to the Corinthians, he cautions against partaking in both the Lord's table and the table of demons, emphasizing the danger of engaging with both domains (1 Corinthians 10:20-21). The spiritual implications of such interactions become evident, illustrating the intricate interplay between good and evil, light and darkness.

A touching narrative unfolds in Acts 16. In the city of Philippi, a girl possessed by a spirit of divination followed Paul and his companions, proclaiming, *"These men are servants of the Most High God, who are proclaiming a way of salvation to you"* (Acts 16:17). While the words appeared true, the source was tainted, for the girl was a pawn in the hands of a deceiving demon. Paul's removal of that demon shattered the bonds of her possession, revealing the manipulative nature of these demons and their attempt to obscure God's truth.

The revelation increases in the Book of Revelation, a prophetic canvas painted with vivid depictions of spiritual warfare and the unfolding of God's plans. The vision of unclean spirits resembling frogs emanating from the mouths of the dragon, the beast, and the false prophet signifies a climactic confrontation between forces of darkness and light (Revelation 16:13-14). These deceitful spirits perform signs, luring and enticing the rulers of the world into a perilous spiritual battle against God Himself.

Throughout the sacred pages of the Bible, the intricate threads of demonology intertwine to form a story that stretches from the beginning of creation to the very end of it. These threads reveal encounters, warnings, and predictions that go beyond what we can see with our eyes and hear with our ears, giving us a glimpse into the unseen spiritual realm. The presence of demons within the pages of the Bible serves as a stark reminder, not only of the existence of evil forces, but also of the unwavering authority of God's power over them. It is within this spiritual realm that we find both the eternal struggle between light and darkness and the resounding love of God for His children.

Now, as we set our course to explore the profound implications of these revelations for your daily life, it's imperative to approach this journey with an open heart and an inquisitive mind. How, you might wonder, do these truths intertwine with your modern existence? What is the relevance of these spiritual battles between God and Satan to your everyday life?

As we delve deeper into the truth of the matter, be prepared for a voyage of discovery that may challenge your preconceptions and prompt a deeper introspection than you are accustomed to. Remember, the journey ahead is one of truth, and it's essential not to allow the forces of deceit to shut the door to the truth that is about to unfold. Keep your heart open, your mind receptive, and together, we will uncover the profound significance of these truths for you, a child loved by God.

Battling the Unseen: Demons and Their Daily Influence on You

This is where the rubber meets the road, as the old phrase goes. This is where your daily decisions in life, what you do and how you do them, along with the influences of darkness, collide.

In the spiritual world, beyond our immediate perception, a battle rages. A battle that transcends the physical, the tangible, and the understood. It's a battle between light and darkness, a battle between God and Satan, a battle against the unseen forces that seek to infiltrate our lives, minds, and spirits. This is the battle against demons and their daily influence on us.

Demons are a reality that has been woven into the tapestry of human existence since the beginning. In Genesis 3:22, God says, *"Look, the human beings have become like us, knowing both good and evil"*. That knowledge wasn't some mystical outside influence. That choice, that decision that forever changed the course of mankind, was internal. It gave Satan access to us. Just as God is in spirit and lives in those that choose Him, so does Satan. Our knowledge of evil comes from within us. It comes from demons sent to destroy us using whatever means possible. Whether or not we choose to acknowledge their existence, they are there, lurking in the shadows and whispering their deceitful lies into our unconscious minds.

Picture this: a brand new day, the sun's gentle rays painting a canvas of endless possibilities. Yet, as you step into your daily routine, you remain blissfully unaware of the invisible forces at play, molding your thoughts, emotions, and actions. Maybe you snap at someone for a minor offense or impatiently cut in line, all seemingly typical in our daily hustle. What you might not realize is that demons are masters of disguise, seamlessly assimilating into the routine of life's commotion. They prey on our weaknesses, exploit our fears, and toy with our desires, working their manipulation from deep within us.

Their influence is subtle; a whisper here, a nudge there. It's the persistence of that thought, telling you to hold on to your anger, nurse your grudges, and let resentment fester. The self-doubt that creeps in when you least expect it, eroding your confidence and undermining your potential. It's the insidious temptation that lures you toward destructive behaviors, convincing you that just one more (fill in the blank) won't hurt. Demons thrive on chaos, confusion, and division, sowing seeds of discord within our relationships, our communities, and even within ourselves.

But the battle against these unseen foes is not a lost cause. It's a battle that requires vigilance, awareness, and a deeper understanding of the spiritual forces at play. It's a battle that compels us to seek the truth, to strengthen our connection with God, and to fortify our hearts and minds against their influence.

Throughout history, stories of exorcisms, of individuals casting out demons, have echoed across time. These tales remind us we have a choice in overcoming their grip. Yet, we fight the battle in the daily choices we make, the thoughts we entertain, and the actions we take.

I have witnessed incredibly powerful demons and even commanders in Satan's army. I've encountered weaker demons and even repentant ones before God. There was a point in my journey where the remaining demons refused to leave. God had issued commands, yet they stubbornly resisted, defying His orders. He issued one final decree, "Any demon found when I arrive will face judgment." Panic surged among the demons to escape while they could, but for many, it was already too late.

When God's immense presence materialized, it sent waves of fear throughout the demons. He blocked further exits and started a judicial process for each and every one. *"Demon of criticism, what crimes have you committed against the creation?"* God's voice resonated powerfully. "My task was to influence criticism and demean others within the creation." *"How did you fulfill this role?"* God questioned. "I accomplished it by making him believe he was less worthy. I attacked his self-worth and made him doubt his value compared to those around him. This prompted him to belittle and scorn people nearby to boost his own sense of self-worth." God listened, then replied in a calm authoritative voice, *"For your crimes against the creation, I sentence you to..."* and God rendered judgment upon the demon.

The next demons came forward one by one. *"What are your crimes against the creation?"* and they would confess. Demon after demon, God issued judgment, each based on specific charges. Some He called by name, revealing His prior knowledge of them before they chose to serve Satan. A few rebellious demons refused to approach God and defied Him. *"Come before Me now!"* God commanded, and not one could deny His authority. Some displayed astonishing defiance, spewing hate toward God in their last moments.

Yet others approached God in repentance. A couple pleaded for mercy. He responded, *"You come before me now, seeking mercy and forgiveness. You seek it now only because it is your time for judgment. Had you come to me before, I would have granted it. I'm sorry, but you will be judged for your crimes against the creation,"* and He delivered judgment to them.

The judgements varied and the punishment for their crimes was not all the same. For some, their existence within the creation ended. For others, He created a realm of darkness and exiled them to eternal solitude within it. I saw it as an isolation prison cell floating in the darkness of space, far away from any life. As for the more rebellious and obstinate demons, He crafted a small space infused with a fragment of His light and love. They were encased in God's love for eternity, an agonizing existence for those who sought darkness.

Once, I witnessed a captain facing judgment before God. His crime against the creation was the orchestration of demons among individuals. He manipulated one person's vulnerabilities to complement another's, using their weaknesses to create a destructive interaction. I observed this scheme play out in the lives of people seeking healing and embracing God. For instance, the demon of lust in one person is linked with the demon of insecurity in another. "Desire me, want me," whispered one demon. In response, the other echoed, "I crave you. I want you desperately." This coordinated pairing by the captain aimed to shatter the lives of both people.

These calculated attacks brought two spirits together in a connection destined to fail. Rooted not in love, but in darkness, these destructive connections left the individuals emotionally ravaged, nurturing more hate and bitterness than before. The pain arising from these connections drove them further from God and His love. This was merely a glimpse into the strategies a captain in Satan's army orchestrates for the destruction of God's people within the creation.

Later, as I transformed into an instrument that God could employ to expel demons from individuals, my ability to see and understand them in the spirit expanded significantly. We've all watched movies featuring that sinister laugh, the one that sends shivers down your spine. Initially, I would sense their presence and then search for them. I could perceive their attempts to conceal themselves hiding down in the darkness that a person carries. Their presence is a kind of darkness that defies any description I've ever encountered.

When I found them, they almost always started laughing. It was a mocking laugh aimed at me and the person they had been tormenting. They would taunt the person, saying things like, 'What a fool, haha-

hahahaha,' 'You were so easy to manipulate, hahaha. You're stupid and can't live without me. You need me! Nobody will want you without me, hahaha.' The taunting and sinister laughter would continue until they left the person, usually accompanied by a loud scream.

In the beginning, I didn't understand how they could communicate through me. It was just as confusing for me as it might be for you reading this and trying to grasp the spiritual truth. God had allowed me to see the darkness so that I could bear witness to it. He wanted me to recognize the enemy for who they were because I would fight against them.

For some individuals, I would ask, 'Do you want to hear what they are saying?' Most of the time, they wanted to know, and the demons would reveal how they had terrorized their lives. Yet, for some, they just wanted them out. But overall, I didn't enjoy giving the demons a voice to torment people anymore. I understood it was a season of learning for me, but as God started granting me more authority, the demons taunted me instead.

"Son of God, what are you doing here?" they would mock. "Son of God, go somewhere else." They tried to mimic the voice of God in order to deceive me. "Son, you've done well, rest," just as I was about to confront a larger demon hiding in the shadows. "Son, I am proud of you. That is enough for today," they would say. Their deceptions were frequent in the early stages, yet the more familiar you become with your Father's voice, the weaker their influence over you becomes.

I had learned a method to distinguish whether it was demons attempting to deceive me or genuinely God speaking to me. One question consistently unveiled the truth: "Do you love Jesus Christ?" This is the sole question of verification when hearing voices in the spiritual world. It's incredibly challenging to discern initially because the voices are faint, and THEY WILL UNDOUBTEDLY AND ABSOLUTELY TRY TO TRICK YOU. No human born on this earth is exempt from their deceit and lies.

I had a friend who was just starting to hear God's voice. I shared with her the single question that serves as the only test for a voice heard in the spirit. Later, she informed me she heard God and asked Him the question. His response was, "Jesus Christ is my son." She found contentment in the answer and accepted the guidance. However, something still felt off to her, so she asked me to confirm the answer she was given. She assured me that the answer was good, indicating it must have been God's voice she heard.

I asked her to repeat the question to me, "Do you love Jesus Christ?" she replied. Did the voice answer that question? I asked. She stumbled over her words and repeated the response she heard: "Jesus Christ is my son." Does that response relate to love, I inquired? Gradually, the reality set in, and she felt disheartened. "Don't feel bad," I comforted her. Demons have perfected the art of deception over thousands of years and are experts in the game.

The simplicity of the question lies in love. God will answer the question unhesitatingly and without reservation until you learn to recognize His voice. "Jesus Christ is my son, whom I love with all that I am," He has answered me. "I love Jesus Christ, my son, more deeply than you can understand," He responded on other occasions. Love, love is the only acceptable answer from God.

Demons are entirely incapable of expressing love, and they wouldn't even consider lying about love because of the fear of immediate judgment from God. Therefore, they will try various ways to avoid the subject, but they can never say "I love Jesus Christ" under any circumstances.

As God granted me more authority over them, they grew quieter in their harassment, hiding in fear of being discovered within a person. Their taunting towards me faded into obscurity as they hid within the darkness. Simply removing a demon doesn't significantly impact Satan's overall purpose, as that demon merely moves from one person to another, or even back to the original person, if we leave the door open. Let's revisit Matthew 12:43-45 once more:

"When an evil spirit leaves a person, it goes into the desert, seeking rest but finding none. Then it says, 'I will return to the person I came from.' So it returns and finds its former home empty, swept, and in order. Then the spirit finds seven other spirits more evil than itself, and they all enter the person and live there. And so that person is worse off than before. That will be the experience of this evil generation."

This passage highlights that demons tend to move around once they are removed from a person. So, what caused these demons to change their behavior when they were uncovered within a person? Well, it was the fact that God had granted me the authority to send the demons that were removed to Him for judgment. This shift in God's tactics transformed their actions from mere taunting and laughter into a grave matter of life and death for them. The prospect of facing judgment before God was now their worst fear, and it completely altered their attitude.

There was a woman whom God had placed in my path. She was a devout atheist, and if God came up, I could sense the hate and anger welling up within her. This woman suffered from anxiety, depression, and fear of everything around her. She had many tattoos and had lived a challenging life by most standards.

On a slight side note, there are actually demons whose sole job is to encourage people to mark up their bodies. You were created perfect in God's image, and these entities want you to deface His creation. It's the equivalent of taking the Mona Lisa and throwing paint over the top of it. There's no judgment in this, as many people have tattoos, but it illuminates what is going on spiritually.

One day, we were scheduled to meet up, but she messaged me saying a panic attack was starting, and she didn't think she could come. I assured her it was no problem and that we could still meet. She had told me before about her anxiety attacks and how she used to take medication for them. The medication would help calm her down.

Having seen what God had revealed to me spiritually up until this point, I was deeply curious to uncover what lay behind an anxiety attack. She came over, visibly shaken and nervous. All she wanted to do was sit on the couch, curled up into a ball. Rocking back and forth, she tightly wrapped her arms around her knees, hugging them tightly to her chest.

I sat next to her, but after 3-4 minutes, I wasn't feeling anything at all. Normally, when I'm near someone emotionally distressed, I sense their turbulent emotions within minutes. I was puzzled. How could someone experiencing such an emotionally intense event as an anxiety attack not reveal any actual emotions attached to it? Then, I requested her permission (by that point, God had instructed me I couldn't connect with people without their prior permission) to explore what she was going through. She nodded yes, unable to speak because of her heightened anxiety.

I closed my eyes, and within mere moments, I began to see and feel the presence of countless demons rejoicing in her suffering. In a matter of seconds, I experienced a disturbing sensation of great pleasure and satisfaction. These demons were rejoicing in her suffering. As I looked into the darkness within her, they hastily scattered away like rats fleeing from the light. This sight left me astonished. What she had been going through, her torment, misery, and anxiety, was nothing more than the result of these demons emerging from the shadows to torture her.

In less than two minutes, her state shifted, and she became calm. We engaged in a regular conversation, leaving her speechless as to how. This was unprecedented for her, as her anxiety attacks typically persisted for at least a day and sometimes stretched to 2-3 days. Yet, this episode had lasted only 5 minutes from its onset.

At some point in her life, the demons had convinced her that there was no God and she completely rejected His existence. She then became fair game for them. With the denial of God, on what authority could she keep them from entering and tormenting her? Where could she seek help from when she had turned her back on the very One that could save her? Rejecting God leaves one utterly powerless against Satan. He gains complete dominion over you and your life. Darkness and burdens will envelop your existence, leading to consequences even graver beyond this life.

Later that same evening, I started to see the demons and heard them mockingly speaking about her. "Stay away from her, Son of God. She won't be able to get rid of even one of us. We control her. She belongs to us," they taunted. On hearing this, she became even more frightened, but God had a message of hope for her:

"A thief sneaks into your home to steal, plunder, and destroy what is yours. They do this quietly at night when you are not alert. But now you know the thief is there. You have discovered their presence in your home, and only the owner of the house has the power to ask the thief to leave.

When the owner of a house comes back and finds the inside damaged and the thief is still there, they don't invite the thief to dine with them. Instead, the owner calls the police, who have the authority to remove the thief hiding in the darkness and give the house back to the rightful owner.

I have shown you the thief who has wrecked your home. You, and only you, have the power to remove the darkness that causes destruction".

After witnessing the truth, the woman felt terrified. The demons' words were accurate. She didn't want to remove even a single one of them. She made the choice to keep living with the influence of Satan, letting him influence her life. It was deeply painful to watch this reality unfold before me, but this is how God operates. He reveals the truth, yet each of us must decide whether or not to follow Him.

Casting Shadows: The Demons of Magic

This division holds a special place within Satan's ranks, composed of the smartest and most intimate associates of Satan. What makes them stand out? The level of knowledge and intricate coordination they are tasked with is truly challenging. Once they establish a connection with an individual, their role involves coordinating signs and presenting social evidence to assert their status as a formidable supernatural power. However, it's crucial to clarify that these demons lack the ability to foresee the future, something reserved solely for God. Instead, their realm of understanding encompasses the present and the past.

What they do to make you believe they can predict future events is a sleight of hand. A little deceit mixed in with the mastery of human behavior and past patterns. Remember my friend that the witch warned me about? The one who was going to steal a large sum of money from me? This is how they 'predicted' the future on that.

Darkness surrounded the friend who was taking care of the business inventory. A 'friend' who was a prostitute befriended her and wanted to be a part of the business. At the right time, this 'friend' took all the inventory and wiped the business clean. Who has the influence in persuading someone to act a certain way? All the demons do is influence behavior. Some people are more susceptible to this influence than others. A person who has accepted God would not be as susceptible as someone living in the darkness.

The demons in the magic division are often wrong. They can't influence everyone every time. Maybe the person decides to do what is right, making their predictions incorrect. The witch had told me that when the predictions didn't come true; it was her fault for doing something different. The lie she was told by her demons was that there is a lesson to be learned in everything, and the event didn't happen so she could grow spiritually. It is a massive and dark operation that Satan runs on the magic side of things. Information about deceased relatives, ones that are still alive, and possible behavioral patterns of those around that person must be relayed quickly and accurately to deceive the person inquiring.

I can always tell when someone has opened themselves to magic. Just by consulting a witch for a reading or cleansing, it gives the demons from this special division access. Walking into that place and opening that door allows a heavy darkness to enter. This person is much more open to letting me connect with them so they can see a path forward. They have been so confused spiritually that they have crossed barriers most would not. Almost immediately, I feel that heavy darkness and mention to them they have done tarot readings, which is usually a deep secret for most. They are shocked, and initially believe it's all connected within the magic realm. God always shines light into that darkness right away, and they quickly realize that God and magic are completely opposing forces.

Demons Within the Animal Kingdom

Let's briefly delve into this topic, as I've witnessed evil influences in animals, raising questions about the subject. Mark 5:11-13 clearly illustrates this: *"There happened to be a large herd of pigs feeding on the hillside nearby. 'Send us into those pigs,' the spirits begged. 'Let us enter them.' So Jesus gave them permission. The evil spirits came out of the man and entered the pigs, and the entire herd of about 2,000 pigs plunged down the steep hillside into the lake and drowned."* This passage serves as confirmation that approximately 2,000 animals were indeed influenced by demons. And let us not overlook the instance of Satan speaking through a serpent in Genesis 3.

I have a friend who recently chose to follow God and dedicate her life to serving Him. One evening, she left Walmart, walking toward her house. Having just sold something, she carried a month's worth of salary in her purse. A pack of 6-8 dogs started following her in the darkness. Even though she was heading to the same house she had grown up in, she had never experienced this before. The dogs chased her, barking and growling. They cornered her against a fence, closing off any escape route. In response, she shouted and swung her purse at their menacing faces. One dog seized her purse and made a run for it, with the other dogs quickly following suit and running off.

She found herself alone and in shock. Not only did she desperately need that money to cover impending bills, but she had unexpectedly become the target of an orchestrated animal attack! Fortunately, a Good Samaritan on a bicycle noticed her distress. She explained the dogs had snatched her purse and fled. Swiftly, the bystander rode after the dogs, bravely using his bike as a shield to drive them away, and managed to retrieve her torn purse. Remarkably, he was able to recover the stolen money as well.

During the turbulent year when I was robbed and nearly murdered, a heartwarming connection formed between me and an affectionate dog named Cloe at one orphanage I visited regularly. Despite over 50 people surrounding her at all times, she would excitedly run to me anytime I was around. It was a beautiful expression of our special bond. I'd shower her with hugs and affection to remind her of how loved she was. Cloe had spent seven years in that orphanage, making her an astute and beloved member.

One day, as I arrived at the orphanage, she didn't appear to greet me as she always had before. My inquiry led to the director informing me that Cloe had tragically been run over and had passed away within the confined compound, which was barely spacious enough for a car to maneuver. The news was heart-wrenching, and I couldn't help but question the motive behind her death. Cloe had survived seven years without incident, and she was astutely aware of vehicles.

Approximately three months after Cloe's death, I formed another connection with a dog at a property where I frequently stayed. This dog was the smallest of its litter, displaying fragility and humility. He became my loyal companion, never straying from my side, no matter where I went on the property. On a particular occasion, I anticipated visiting the property with excitement, looking forward to reuniting with my little friend. I had even purchased a doggy jacket to shield him from the cold, as well as flea powder and nutritional food, to ensure his well-being while I was away. Before my visit, I messaged the property's neighbor to inquire about the little dog's condition, only to receive the devastating news that he too, had met a tragic end. A truck backing up had fatally run him over, in the identical manner in which Cloe had perished.

In the wake of these heart-wrenching losses, I couldn't help but question the motives behind these tragedies. Both Cloe and the little dog had been cherished and loved, and their untimely deaths left me with a lingering sense of unease. The striking similarity in the manner of their passing only deepened my sense of wonder. As I continued my journey deeper into the battles between God and Satan, these incidents would become constant reminders of the unseen forces at play in our lives.

Cultivating Darkness: The Expansion of Demonic Influence in One's Life

I've witnessed varying degrees of darkness within individuals, spanning an entire spectrum with distinct levels of influence in each person. Guided by God, my journey aimed to uncover the truth: why do some people carry a much heavier darkness than others? What divides heavy darkness from light, and why do demons affect some more than others? The answer lies in the <u>choices</u> we make.

From birth, we inherit the basic understanding of good and evil, a decision made long ago by Adam and Eve that has shaped our trajectory. Initially, seeing the prevalent darkness, I harbored a grudge towards these two figures. Why should we all pay the price for their choice? God, in His boundless love, reassured me, saying, *"Every human after Adam and Eve would have made the same choice."* Thus, our shared path in sin endures not because of their sole actions but because subsequent generations would have made the identical decision to eat the forbidden fruit.

Returning to the topic of choices, our lives are filled with everyday moments that offer us the chance to decide. Do we cut someone off in traffic? Is that an act of love or hate? Do we raise our voice to someone who has made a mistake? Is that response rooted in love or hate? When faced with the presence of conflict, do we opt for violence or choose the path of love? When presented with the opportunity, do we embrace love or surrender to selfishness? Each of these instances becomes a crossroads, presenting us with a choice over light and darkness.

This is how darkness is invited into our lives, by consciously choosing hate over love. At first, these choices may seem inconspicuous, but they open the door for a demon to enter. One choice leads to another, and soon, darkness spreads like a suffocating fog, obscuring the essence of our true nature: love.

Imagine a map of Houston, Texas stretched before you. As you orient the map northward, draw a dividing line. On the left stands God, while Satan occupies the right. Inevitably, you'll journey to the northernmost point, beginning from the map's southernmost tip. Every intersection poses a choice: turn left towards God or right towards Satan. On this journey, there are no GPS or road signs; your internal voice becomes your compass.

As you begin your journey northward from the southernmost part, you're faced with a decision at every crossroad, whether to turn left or right. While traveling north, your choices at each intersection, guided by your inner voice, will determine whether you navigate through the shaded or illuminated sections of the map. If you allow yourself to be led northward without actively choosing, you'll find yourself on the toll roads of the map's darker side. This path exacts a toll on your life, leaving you tired and beaten up by the time you reach your destination. To travel north in the light requires purposeful and intentional effort, as it's not the default route anymore.

The choices you make in every moment of your day determine the influence that will shape your life. These aren't the choices that immediately lead from cutting someone off in traffic to the urge to commit murder. Rather, it's a gradual process, a slow darkening of the spirit that unfolds over years and even decades. Do you find more love and joy in your life at 30 than you did at 16? Does life appear even more beautiful to you at 60 compared to when you were 30?

Or do you sense a heavier presence, a deeper darkness than you recall experiencing at a younger age? These are significant questions that each of us in this creation must ask ourselves.

What serves as the benchmark against which you measure your inner light? I've witnessed individuals walking in darkness while declaring God's light guides them. How could they have fallen under such a deception? When did these demons infiltrate their lives? "Well, of course, I'm not as joyful as I was at 15, but that's just how life goes," they declare. Yes, that's life, altered by the choices that have darkened our path and allowed the influence of Satan to contaminate the light. God doesn't desire <u>any</u> of His children to live in the darkness, but He permits it if they choose to do so. What criteria do you employ to assess the direction you're headed? What acts as your GPS locator to discern your position on the map of life?

Demons may not be visible to the human eye, but their profound influence casts a shadow over our lives. It's there when we unconsciously choose hate over love, when we prioritize the pursuit of this world over nurturing a relationship with God, and when we allow the influence of fear to dictate our actions. Demons thrive on our vulnerabilities, exploiting our doubts, and taking advantage of our disconnection from our Creator.

Yet, as we navigate the roads of this life, we must remain steadfast in our understanding that the battle against demons is not an isolated struggle. God is always patiently waiting by our side to help us in any and every circumstance. All we have to do is turn to Him. "God, I need your help" is all that needs to be whispered.

In this journey, the quest for the truth takes on immense significance. Daily choosing the path illuminated by God, we weaken the grip of Satan's forces. It is through our conscious choices to seek God, seek His will, that we transform ourselves into warriors of light, challenging the demons that seek to lead us astray.

With each new sunrise you are blessed to see, embrace God's will in your life. Approach every decision with mindfulness, aware of the influences that seek to contaminate your spirit. By acknowledging and passionately resisting the daily onslaught of demonic influences, you allow a space for God to work in your life. A life lived in agreement with love, truth, and the divine purpose that God has for you.

Having dedicated ample time and energy to shedding light on the ways demons exert their influence in our daily lives, it's time for a shift in focus. Let's now delve into the intriguing realm of how God imparts His guidance to His beloved children through various channels of communication.

The Concept of Sin:
Understanding It Better

N ow, let's briefly delve into what sin truly entails and why God consistently rescues His people from its clutches. God authors every life born on this Earth. But how does He author life? During the early stages of my healing process, God revealed this to me as I sought the true meaning of life. The insight was so profound that it moved me to tears.

Every single life born, without exception, is authored by God. He takes a fragment of Himself and places it into every newborn. Life on Earth is brought into existence through the convergence of three origins: a man, a woman, and God. Even children born into tragic circumstances or abandoned at birth are lives authored by God. He confirmed that whenever sperm and eggs unite, He authors that life. He respects the decisions of all people and their freedom to make their own choices, even if they are not the wisest decisions.

God revealed He takes a portion of Himself, His light, His love, and embeds it within the fusion of eggs and semen. The revelation of this connection with God's love was so powerful that words cannot adequately convey it. Every person born carries a piece of God's love within them. His love functions as the life-generating power source for everyone on Earth. He revealed we are all profoundly connected through His love, as our heavenly Father has given a piece of Himself to create life within us. Witnessing and experiencing the source of love necessary to bring forth life throughout the world was truly awe-inspiring. Its depth and magnitude are beyond our human understanding.

Knowing where we come from helps us understand what sin really means. Sin isn't a rule given by God to control His creation. Instead, sin is like an idea, a thought about who we aren't supposed to be. Sin is the opposite of where we should go and what we should do because of Who our Creator is. Let me explain this in other terms.

Imagine you got a Bugatti La Voiture Noire, a car that's worth about 13 million U.S. Dollars. Even if you're not a car expert, you can understand that a 13-million-dollar car is incredibly special. The La Voiture Noire is an extremely limited-edition car, with only one unit ever produced. Its exclusivity and rarity significantly drive up its value.

You own this unique and almost invaluable vehicle, and you decide to drive it to the mountains right away. However, you're not sticking to the smooth, curvy roads they made the car for. Instead, you're taking it off the road, onto rough terrain. As you encounter the first muddy pothole, the front fender cracks and the rim bends. Then you step on the gas and speed up, causing rocks to hit the paint and chip it.

Then you see a really steep hill and try to climb it, but you only make it halfway. The car slips back and hits a rock, damaging its rear end and breaking the tail lights. Later, you speed up down a narrow road where tree branches scratch the paint and dent the bodywork. When you're done off-roading, the car looks worn out and beaten. Its value has dropped by millions, and no one would even buy it anymore.

As you navigate the challenging terrain, every bump, pothole, and obstacle leaves its mark on the car, diminishing its value and appearance. In a way, our journey through life parallels this experience. Just like the car, you were created completely unique and valuable. Each one of us is as rare as a limited-edition masterpiece, unlike anyone else in the world. However, sin, in all its forms, acts like the pothole that messes up the rim, the rocks that hit the paint, and the steep hill climb that should be avoided. Sin damages our pristine design, leaving us feeling unworthy and less valuable. Sin is what God wants us to steer clear of in order to protect our preciousness. That's the true nature of sin.

Whispers of Grace: God's Desire to Communicate with Us

How does a divine God communicate with a people contaminated by sin? His presence is so Holy and Divine that He must maintain a special distance from the creation. Not only that, but the creation was designed to function independently, with no need for direct intervention from God. Animals have their purpose, plants have their purpose, the sky serves its purpose, and the waters have their designated role. This distinct purpose of everything is to sustain humanity on Earth.

In the beginning, God walked and talked with humanity. He desired to commune and connect with His creation, overflowing with love from every corner of the world. We find this account in Genesis 3:8-13 when God discovered Adam and Eve's actions:

"When the cool evening breezes were blowing, the man and his wife heard the Lord God walking about in the garden. So they hid from the Lord God among the trees. Then the Lord God called to the man, 'Where are you?' He replied, 'I heard you walking in the garden, so I hid. I was afraid because I was naked.'"

It's incredible to understand that God once walked among us. However, this marked the last time God's complete presence could be among His creation. After sin entered and Satan contaminated the world, God had to withdraw His full presence from the earth. His pure essence was incompatible with the sin in humanity.

God's Voice in The Creation:
How He Speaks to Us

The **Bible:** God has given us an incredible tool for hearing His words. This amazing book is a compilation of 66 individual books brought together as one voice for all of humanity to hear. There is nothing that comes even close to the power of these books. Each one represents a time within the creation where God guided His children or corrected them to preserve their life and well being.

People look to the universe, magic stones, candles, spiritual meditation, spiritual guides, and more to find the truth when it has been in front of them all along. Understanding that these stories and lessons from the Bible are thousands of years old and contain incredible accuracy for the time they were written in is no accident.

One of the oldest Bible stories that archaeological evidence has verified is the tale of the destruction of the city of Jericho. The Book of Joshua in the Old Testament mentions the city of Jericho, describing how the city walls fell after the Israelites marched around it for seven days, guided by the Ark of the Covenant. Archaeological excavations at the Jericho site have unveiled evidence of a collapsed city wall dating back to a period consistent with the biblical account, supporting the idea that some form of destruction occurred there in ancient times. The discovery of the fallen walls aligns with the general timeline and context of the story in the Book of Joshua. This event is believed to have taken place around 1400 to 1300 BC (Before Christ), approximately 3,400 to 3,300 years ago from the present day.

In 2 Timothy 3:16, it states, *"All Scripture is inspired by God and is useful to teach us what is true and to make us realize what is wrong in our lives. It corrects us when we are wrong and teaches us to do what is right."*

The Bible is not merely a compilation of stories or ancient records; it is a collection of God's spoken word to us. It's a dialogue of love, where the Creator communicates His wisdom, love, and purpose to His children. In the end, it's not about the age of the words within these sacred pages, nor is it solely about the historical accuracy they may hold. It's about the enduring truth and profound connection they offer to our Creator. The Bible is a living testament to His presence in our journey, offering timeless lessons and unwavering truths for all who will listen.

Messengers of Light:
God's Voice Spoken Through Others

Because of the accumulation of sin we carry (imagine bent rim, dinged paint, damaged body), direct communication with us becomes a challenge for God because of His divinity. That sin, the darkness, acts as a communication barrier between God and us. Visualize a communication conduit with corroded cables, gradually eroded by rust, leading to intermittent signals and, at times, complete signal loss. Nevertheless, there are individuals who have been given the gift of direct communication with God to serve their brothers and sisters. In fact, God gives many gifts to facilitate His communication with His children.

1 Corinthians 12:4-11:

"There are different kinds of spiritual gifts, but the same Spirit is the source of them all. There are different kinds of service, but we serve the same Lord. God works in different ways, but it is the same God who does the work in all of us. A spiritual gift is given to each of us so we can help each other. To one person the Spirit gives the <u>ability to give wise advice</u>; to another the same Spirit gives a <u>message of special knowledge</u>. The same Spirit gives <u>great faith</u> to another, and to someone else the one Spirit gives the <u>gift of healing</u>. He gives one person the <u>power to perform miracles</u>, and another the <u>ability to prophesy</u>. He gives someone else the <u>ability to discern whether a message is from the Spirit of God or from another spirit.</u> Still another person is given the ability to speak in unknown languages, while another is given the <u>ability to interpret what is being said.</u>

It is the one and only Spirit who distributes all these gifts. He alone decides which gift each person should have."

I absolutely must emphasize a critical part of this scripture. By now, you are aware of how Satan deceives even God's followers. *"He gives someone else the ability to discern whether a message is from the Spirit of God or from another spirit."* This insight is crucial to avoiding false prophets who might enter your life or church and start a campaign of misinformation and division, however subtle.

-Matthew 7:15 *"Beware of false prophets who come disguised as harmless sheep but are really vicious wolves."*

-Matthew 24:24 *"For false messiahs and false prophets will rise up and perform great signs and wonders so as to deceive, if possible, even God's chosen ones."*

-1 John 4:1 *"Dear friends, do not believe everyone who claims to speak by the Spirit. You must test them to see if the spirit they have comes from God. For there are many false prophets in the world."*

This is why knowing God's word is so important. He has given us a blueprint, a map of who He is: His love, compassion, mercy, and hope for us all are laid out for us to read. Use this word, the Bible, to discern if what was told to you is correct. Don't rely on feelings and emotions; the enemy can influence those. Instead, use God's word as a light to hold up against the message, advice, and counsel given to you by others.

In the next chapter about "Listening to God," we come to understand that God employs various means to convey His messages to His children. One of these means is through individuals gifted with the ability to hear His voice and serve as messengers of His light. However, not all will listen to God when He speaks.

Listening to God

I vividly recall the very first message I received from God. I was just 16 years old, serving as a volunteer in the sound booth at our newly established church. This quaint congregation had recently found its footing and was making do with a rented, aging building. My role was to occupy the balcony, operating the sound system every Sunday for the worship team and our pastor.

On this Sunday evening, a guest speaker had come to speak at the church for a small, intimate gathering, and I found myself alone in the dimly lit balcony. After the worship service, he approached the small stage and began singling out individuals among the congregation, delivering messages to them. I could sense God's presence, yet I wasn't sure if what was being said was accurate. The advice given to each person sounded wise. Despite being tucked away in the dark balcony, far from everyone else, he suddenly paused, looked up at me, and said, 'You.'

For probably the past year, I had been privately praying for something that nobody else knew about. I hadn't even spoken those private thoughts and prayers. So when the guest speaker paused, looked directly at me, and said, 'You,' my heart started racing. He delivered a deeply personal and impactful message that directly addressed the prayer I had been silently uttering for the past year. In that moment, there was absolutely no doubt that God hears our prayers. And for that 16-year-old boy, another undeniable revelation dawned: God speaks to His children through others.

Messages that God has given to me for others are actually quite varied. Most of the time, they are visual images, followed by a translation that God reveals. Others are conveyed through direct word-for-word communication, and I just start writing them down as God gives them to me. Some are simply translations of dreams people have had. And yes, I've actually had to act out some messages too.

One time, God gave me an image along with a message to deliver to a single mom with two kids. I knew almost nothing about her history, and she had only recently crossed my path. I messaged her, asking if I could visit her home and if we could go for a walk. She agreed, but for the message to be fully expressed, it had to be done at night. I won't deceive anyone about the stress of receiving these messages. Delivering a message from God to someone I didn't know was extremely nerve-wracking in the beginning. I didn't know if they would yell at me, spit at me, hit me, or berate me. Those were the fears I had initially. But I had made a promise to God that I would deliver each and every message.

As we walked through the neighborhood, I was scanning for the right spot. I needed a clear division between light and darkness. I found a tall streetlight with a structure beneath it. The structure, backlit by the light, cast a shadow on the ground, leaving me standing with light on one side and darkness on the other.

She noticed my nervousness and peculiar behavior as I observed the interplay of shadows and light around me. Curiously, she finally asked, "What are you doing?" Unsure of how to explain to this woman what I was up to, I asked her to sit on a bench because I had a message for her.

Her unease quickly matched mine as I positioned myself within the shadow, my entire body concealed from the light. I extended my left hand from the shadow, illuminating it up to my forearm. With my head turned backwards, facing the darkness of the shadow, I delivered God's message.

"My body in the darkness represents your spirit," I said. "You are almost entirely engulfed by darkness, and it's leaving you feeling lost. My hand signifies your effort to reach out for something better. You sense the presence of light, but you're unsure of how to step into it. Now watch." With my head still looking into the darkness and my right hand clenched tightly, I continued, "You must shift your focus, for you're looking back into the darkness." Slowly, I turned my head to face the light where my extended hand was illuminated. I continued, "You have to let go of what you're holding onto in the darkness," as I opened my right hand, releasing a hold in the darkness, and began walking into the light.

She remained utterly silent. The shock was apparent on her face. I didn't know what to say or do, perhaps because it was one of my earlier messages for someone. And maybe that was okay. I understand that when God's message penetrates through the darkness to touch the heart, it's a profoundly impactful moment. After what felt like an eternity of silence, but was actually just a few minutes, she began to talk and open up.

On another occasion, a friend reached out to me because she had experienced two vivid dreams that she could recall in great detail the following morning, prompting her to write them down. The first dream had an obvious message, but the second one puzzled her. This is her second dream:

"When the first dream finished, I transitioned to another dream, one resembling a novel. In this dream, a woman emerged, mistreating me with great rudeness. I stumbled upon her Bible, carelessly discarded in the water, bearing her name. In an urge to retaliate, I contemplated exposing her loss to everyone. As in this dream, losing one's Bible was considered the utmost disgrace. However, God intervened, forbidding me from such an act, as He does not endorse revenge.

Instead, I sent her a picture to show my possession of it, returning the Bible and explaining that I was bound by God's prohibition against taking any further action regarding the discarded Bible. Her reaction was fierce; she heatedly asserted that I had maliciously taken it from the beginning. My abrupt awakening followed, right at the moment she attempted to shatter something over my head."

I sensed a profound message within this dream/vision and encouraged her to seek God for its interpretation. Remarkably, within minutes, God began unveiling the following interpretation to me:

In this dream, the woman represents the authority of the church, while the discarded Bible symbolizes those individuals who have been cast out and stained by their rejection from the church community. Your desire to expose their embarrassment to the world represents Satan's attempt to expose people's shame through the actions of church members, cultivating destructive gossip that damages fragile hearts.

The water, in contrast, symbolizes God, who absorbs the impurity and stains from those who have been cast aside. The returning of the Bible to the lady represents you becoming an instrument of God, helping to bring these lost and discarded hearts back into the church fold.

The woman's violent reaction to you bringing the discarded back represents the presence of Satan within the church, blaming and fiercely attacking those who seek to return and reconnect with God. These attacks, as depicted in your dream, highlight the harsh spiritual challenges faced by those who return to the church, seeking God's love.

God's messages to individuals aren't solely intended for their benefit alone. This particular message was meant for everyone, initially conveyed to a woman and subsequently translated by God through another. This is one of the ways God communicates with His people. It is essential for believers to assess whether such messages align with the teachings of the Bible, if they promote His love for His people, and if they contain truths that resonate with His Word.

God comprehends that we each perceive and receive information differently. He knows precisely how to reach a person's heart. I used to think that messages from God were mostly meant for correcting believers. However, a significant portion of these messages were directed towards people who didn't know God. Trust me, delivering a message that pierces the heart of someone unfamiliar with God is an incredible honor.

I've also delivered messages to people who attend church regularly and proclaim their faith in God, only to have those messages rejected. To this day, the most intense rejection came from a fellow Christian. Her response carried a strong hatred that left me impacted for a couple of days.

This woman had previously received a gentle and loving message of correction from God about a year before. In that message, God revealed an image of her heart as bright and full of light. However, her left arm was full of darkness and she used it to connect with the people around her. The translation was that her heart was motivation for her actions, but the darkness in her arm contaminated her connections with others when she reached out to them.

Although she accepted the message at the moment, she refused to turn to God as the months passed on. God had compassion and patience for her because of the important work she was doing with children. About nine months later, I received another message from God for her, outlining a pathway to healing and freedom from darkness. Regrettably, she outright ignored this message. Then, approximately a year and a half after the initial message, I received a strong written message from God directed at her. The essence of the message was clear: "Turn away from the darkness before it's too late. Seek your loving God's guidance, and He will rescue you from the path to destruction."

Upon receiving the third message, anger consumed her. She protested, "Who are you to tell me I have darkness? All you do is talk about darkness. Maybe you should pray to God"! She declared these messages were not from God, but from Satan himself, asserting that she followed God faithfully and knew nothing about this darkness I kept talking about. The hatred she directed at me was shocking, leaving a profound impact.

She was about to receive a $250,000 donation for a construction project aimed at helping children. The project was set to commence in just seven days. I warned that her refusal to heed God's messages was resulting in the removal of the construction project from her. Her response was dismissive, stating, "Well, I trust God. If it doesn't happen, it's not God's will."

Approximately two days later, I felt an overwhelming presence of God. I sensed His fury. *"How dare she call my voice the voice of Satan! She accuses my son of being a servant of Satan and my words as Satan's words!"* God's anger surged within me. *"How can my children be so lost that they can't even recognize the sound of their Father's voice?"* His anger swiftly turned to sadness as He declared, *"I have withdrawn my blessing from her. She will stumble and fail in her endeavors until she kneels herself before me. Her prideful heart shifts blame to me instead of taking responsibility for her choices."*

I lost contact with her since then. Initially, construction was slated to start four months ago, but it has just been officially canceled. Approximately six weeks after God's declaration, child protective services intervened, removing all the children they had placed with her. There have also been reports of her health deteriorating rapidly. However, it's crucial to understand that the moment she turns to God, He will be there with open arms, waiting to embrace her with His love.

We've all experienced moments when we've drifted away from the embrace of God's love and grace. However, there are times when we find ourselves in a state where we struggle to hear His voice. What happens when the channels of communication seem blocked or faint? What do we do when there isn't a prophet or a messenger in our lives to speak God's voice to us? And what if our own pride prevents us from heeding the messages that come our way? In these moments, we may wonder: how does God continue to communicate His unwavering love to us?

Detours: The Barriers That Guide Us

God's love for us is so immense that He will employ any means possible to reach us while still respecting our free will. He communicates through His written word, others around us, sermons, songs, and even barriers that block our intended paths. Consider the example of the woman who rejected God's messages multiple times. How will He continue to convey His love to her? The answer lies in the barriers that arise in her life, redirecting her towards Him. He seeks to lead her back to His boundless love, mercy, and grace.

She might dismiss the written message brought to her by another person. But what about a $250,000 project that was only a week away from commencing? Contracts were in place, funding donations secured, architects ready, governmental permits granted, and a construction company prepared to begin work. This extensive undertaking, spanning international boundaries and involving significant funds, had come together over six months. Yet, that project, slated to launch in just seven days, was abruptly halted.

In a remarkably brief span of time, a $50,000 material donation pledged by one contributor fell through. A church that had initially committed thousands withdrew its support. Additionally, the primary construction company, set to lead the project, withdrew mere days before initiation.

Those are the barriers and signs that serve as guides to us when we cannot hear God's voice. Don't blame God for the barriers; He is only helping to protect us from the enemy. Instead, stop and ask yourself, "What am I not seeing? What decisions do I need to make? Am I walking in God's will for my life"?

Ephesians 5:17 states: *"Therefore do not be foolish, but understand what the Lord's will is."*

So, as you navigate the path of life, be alert to the surrounding barriers. They may not always be a direct message from God, but when you notice a pattern of barriers hindering your progress, turn to God's word, the Bible, and seek His voice from the nearest source you have. Allow Him to guide you back to His path, where love and compassion overflow.

Although we might encounter seasons of spiritual drought or uncertainty, God's love remains unwavering. He continues to find ways to communicate His love and purpose to us. Our role is to stay open, receptive, and humble, ready to discern His voice in the subtle whispers of life, the wisdom of others, and the timeless truths of His Word. Even when we can't hear Him clearly, we can have faith that God's love always surrounds us, ready to lead us back into the warmth of His embrace.

Satan: Unveiling the Prince of Darkness

In the initial encounters, I witnessed God during His conversations with Satan. God would address Satan, and Satan's responses would often carry an air of indifference, saying, "Yes, God?" When God summoned him. On one occasion, I remember God sternly warning Satan to steer clear of me. God asserted I had been chosen by Him, and Satan was to leave me alone. Shortly after that exchange, an unusual event occurred. They robbed me of a significant amount of money, an unprecedented occurrence in my life. God, fully aware that this act was a direct defiance of His command, summoned Satan before Him without delay.

In a commanding voice, God called for him, *"Satan!"* And promptly, Satan appeared, answering, "Yes, God?" God's response was direct and intense, *"You disobeyed my orders and acted against my son."* However, Satan remained astonishingly nonchalant in the face of God's anger, replying, "Relax, God. Everything is okay. No harm was done."

As God's anger intensified because of Satan's blatant defiance, He demanded that His commands be adhered to within the creation. However, Satan's demeanor revealed a chilling awareness of just how far he could push the boundaries with God; this defiance was just a small part of his overall strategy.

One revelation that I wasn't initially conscious of, until God unveiled it to me, was the ongoing negotiation between God and Satan. These glimpses into their interactions offer a unique insight into their relationship, and the Bible provides us with a window into this intriguing dynamic.

The story unfolds in Job 1:6-12:

"One day the members of the heavenly court came to present themselves before the Lord, and the Accuser, Satan, came with them. 'Where have you come from?' the Lord asked Satan. Satan answered the Lord, 'I have been patrolling the earth, watching everything that's going on.' Then the Lord asked Satan, 'Have you noticed my servant Job? He is the finest man in all the earth. He is blameless—a man of complete integrity. He fears God and stays away from evil.'

Satan replied to the Lord, 'Yes, but Job has good reason to fear God. You have always put a wall of protection around him and his home and his property. You have made him prosper in everything he does. Look how rich he is! But reach out and take away everything he has, and he will surely curse you to your face!'

'All right, you may test him,' the Lord said to Satan. 'Do whatever you want with everything he possesses, but don't harm him physically.' So Satan left the Lord's presence."

The Bible indeed portrays instances of communication and negotiation between God and Satan regarding Satan's influence within the creation. It's crucial to remember that these events took place thousands of years ago, at a time when Satan's influence within people was not as pervasive as it is today.

During an evening stroll, engaged in conversation with God, He unveiled a deeper truth to me. He disclosed that the necessity to negotiate with Satan exists because of his prevailing influence over the creation. God reaffirmed to me His unwavering authority over the creation, emphasizing His absolute control over the universe. However, He acknowledged Satan possesses the capacity to generate repercussions stemming from God's actions within the creation.

Thus, until the time of judgment, God navigates His decisions regarding the creation with careful wisdom, recognizing the intricate balance that must be maintained.

On another contemplative walk, God illustrated the necessity of removing Satan from His presence prior to the creation of Earth. Satan's darkening presence had become heavy, too difficult for God to be around. God conveyed that banishing Satan from the heavens was an agonizing decision, filled with difficulty. As God shared this revelation, Satan unexpectedly appeared, expressing his desire to present his perspective on the matter. True to His nature of truth, God permitted Satan to speak his version of events. This interaction highlighted God's commitment to truth and His willingness to allow even opposing voices to be heard, offering a profound glimpse into His great love for the creation.

I heard Satan proclaim he was the victim in all of this. God had cast him away like unwanted garbage. He seethed with anger at God for removing him from His presence, feeling entitled to compensation. I questioned why we had to listen to Satan. God assured me it was acceptable to let him speak, after which he would depart. Satan defended himself during that walk and then left. Satan consistently referred to me as "the boy" and was incensed by my presence during many of these conversations. "Why is the boy here, God?" he would snarl.

As the majority of demons had been removed from me by God, Satan's tactics changed. I found myself in a session where a highly ranked official of Satan began communicating with me. I commanded him to leave in the name of God, but he persisted. "Who do you think allowed me to be here?" he arrogantly retorted. I realized God had granted him permission to be there and attempt to recruit me.

I felt the authority of this demon and his heavy darkness. For hours, he attempted to recruit me with a barrage of lies and deceit. He questioned God's love for me, asserting that God permitted his access due to neglect. This demon claimed they could provide what God wouldn't on Earth. He sowed seeds of doubt, suggesting that God was fearful of the creation, thus explaining His absence here. "God is hiding in the heavens away from the creation" he would say.

When his previous attempts failed, he resorted to trying to buy me off. "Do you want a million dollars?" he asked. "I could get you a hot young blond-haired beauty that would make everyone else envy you. Success? A nice car? A nice house? I'm authorized to get you anything you want." He persisted with these offers for hours on end, but eventually left in defeat. The prolonged onslaught from Satan and his dominions dismayed me. In the following weeks and months, I would question God about these experiences and their purpose. God would eventually reveal the reason (which I will share with you a little later), but it was exhausting and disheartening.

The Bible recounts instances of Satan employing similar tactics. Notably, in the Gospels of Matthew and Luke, Satan tempts Jesus by offering Him the world's kingdoms. The verses from the following passages describe this event.

Matthew 4:8-9, "Again, the devil took him to a very high mountain and showed him all the kingdoms of the world and their splendor. 'All this I will give you,' he said, 'if you will bow down and worship me.'"

Luke 4:5-7, "The devil led him up to a high place and showed him in an instant all the kingdoms of the world. And he said to him, 'I will give you all their authority and splendor; it has been given to me, and I can give it to anyone I want to. If you worship me, it will all be yours.'"

These verses portray the temptation that Jesus faced during His forty days of fasting and preparation in the wilderness. It's an example of how Satan attempts to entice us by offering things of this world.

However, Jesus firmly rejected Satan's offer and responded with Scripture, affirming His commitment to worship and serve God alone. This event showcases Satan's tactics to recruit everyone who is born into this world. Not even Jesus, God's son, was exempt from Satan's attempts at worldly temptation.

Wrestling with the Devil: Direct
Encounters with Satan

The first time Satan came directly at me, I was alone in the gym, working out. I felt an extremely dark presence and knew right away that this was a darkness unlike any I had felt with the demons or commanders of Satan's army in the past. He was direct and to the point. "You and I, boy, can do great things together. Come, let's destroy this creation together. You have a magnificent gift that shouldn't be wasted. I will use your gift to sway people towards my ways. Let's work together." I told Satan I wasn't interested, and he left.

After the encounter, I cried out to God, "Why?" How and why does Satan have access to me? It drove me crazy that the Prince of Darkness could show up and start a conversation with me. God remained silent on the subject for now. A couple of weeks later, I was in my kitchen when Satan showed up again for a conversation.

He started telling me how the creation was his and that God had lost His grip on it. He was proud and arrogant about his accomplishments. "Come join me," he exclaimed. "I will use you to accomplish great things. They will know your name throughout the earth." I cried out to God again, but this time in the middle of the conversation. I was so tired of hearing Satan's recruitment lines, and I had already chosen God hundreds of times leading up to this point. Each time a powerful demon had come up and tried persuading me to let him stay, I had to choose God. Hundreds of times through this process, I had chosen God, and yet Satan still had access to talk to me.

This time, God showed up instantly. He was furious at Satan. *"Satan!"* He yelled in a controlled, authoritative tone. *"I have told you to stay away from my son,"* He proclaimed. Satan wasn't very affected. "The boy and I were just having a little conversation, God. What are you worried about? Are you afraid the boy will choose me over you?" Satan continued, "Admit that what I have done with your creation is impressive! I don't have any of the power you have, but I have taken control over the creation from you. Imagine what I could have done with your power!" he proudly boasted.

God responded, *"It is true you are very intelligent. You could have done so much with your existence, but your arrogance and pride got in the way. Now, if you talk to my son again without permission, I will judge 50 demons. Let's see how much you value the lives of the ones that follow you."* That was the last time Satan would communicate with me directly outside of God's presence.

What I didn't know at the time was that Satan was facing a tough decision regarding what to do with me. He had a better understanding than I did of the direction God was leading me in. By this point, God had removed all the demons from me, leaving Satan without influence or presence within me. In hindsight, I realized this was akin to sending troops to conquer territory without having accurate intelligence about the current situation. Satan's presence within us grants him access to real-time information about God's activities. A demon reports on God's work within a specific person, and Satan must swiftly deploy countermeasures to thwart God's plans.

With no demonic presence in me, Satan was unaware of God's specific plans for me, but he recognized they were going to be detrimental to his own interests. Though the next move was a risky gamble that could come at a significant cost, Satan deemed it worthwhile. He had tried sending demons to taunt me, commanders to bribe me, and even made personal visits to sway me, but he had exhausted almost all of his options. There was only one option available to him. Satan made the fateful decision to order my removal from the earth.

"Once created, always created," God told me once. Satan couldn't kill me, but he could remove me from the earth. The attack was violent and fierce, but God intervened and protected me. Satan would not decide who lived or died on this earth. That was God's decision. There was a severe price to pay for Satan's attempt to remove me. He lost one of his best friends and generals in his army when God issued judgment for his act of evil and absolute defiance of His orders.

The Dark Mirror:
Satan's Reflection on The Creation

Months after witnessing the judgment for the attempted murder, God allowed Satan to share his perspective on our existence with me. The following narrative is Satan's account, as granted by God, so the truth of both sides may be known:

In this vision, I saw a vast expanse of space, illuminated by a solitary white light. I discerned it as God in solitude, surrounded by nothingness. Gradually, God created Satan, one of His earliest creations, instilling him with remarkable intelligence, just slightly below God's own. Following this, God initiated the creation of angels. Yet, within the heavens, a dispute emerged. Satan opposed God's practice of creating a life without choice. He questioned the appropriateness of creating beings who lacked the autonomy to choose their existence. Furthermore, once created, God, in His love, refrained from terminating any creation, unable to bring Himself to destroy that which He had brought into being. God is a creator of life, an artist.

In time, a tension grew in the heavens. This discord upset God, leading Him to create darkness, a realm where those averse to His creation could dwell. This introduced an element of "choice" for the beings created. Subsequently, Satan, along with his followers, found themselves banished from the heavens, cast into this realm of darkness. This was the first creation of God.

Later, God created the Earth. This creation differed significantly from the first. Upon its completion, God called out to Satan, saying, "Look at what I have done, Satan. This is going to be different. Come back and join me." (I sensed a sincere call from God, beckoning this group back from the darkness into His love.) Satan seethed with fury and demanded to know why God was continuing to create more life. God earnestly pleaded with Satan, explaining that this creation was distinct and begging him to join in this new venture. <u>This was the second creation of God.</u>

Satan and his followers, who were cast into darkness, set out to destroy the second creation. It was a battle between the first creation and the second creation, a conflict that continues to this very day. Witnessing His two creations engaged in such conflict, God's heart was shattered. The situation brought immense distress to Him, as His desire had always been for all beings to live in love and peace. Now, He finds Himself in the role of a referee between the two creations. Though reluctant to cause harm to any aspect of His creations, He understands circumstances will require a decision.

That was the end of the vision.

What I've shared is what Satan revealed to me when God permitted him access. By this point, you are familiar with Satan's identity and significance. I won't provide any commentary on the authenticity of his narrative, as God instructed me to recount what I witnessed and leave it to His people to discern the truth for themselves.

The Ultimatum: Keys to the Kingdom or Destruction of The Creation

I did not believe it when I saw it the first time, nor the second time, the third time, and not even so much the fourth time. However, by the fifth and sixth time, I realized it could be true. Satan has said many times, "I want to be destroyed. God, will you end my existence now? Finish this!" Satan is woven into the creation, so God cannot eliminate him without destroying the Earth.

I was suspicious of the motive, believing it could be a lie to deceive me. Time and time again, I've heard Satan tell God, "Destroy me." He claims God won't do it. Satan's existence is miserable, and he doesn't want to continue existing. I witnessed Satan presenting the Earth to God, declaring that humanity was beyond redemption. One of my last witnessed interactions between God and Satan, there was an ultimatum given by Satan.

In this recent encounter, Satan boldly declared, "At last, the final prophecy unfolds," as he stood before God. He followed with a startling demand, "These people are not redeemable! Give me the keys to the kingdom, or destroy the creation."

God believes His people are still redeemable, and He will never hand the keys of the kingdom over to Satan. However, Satan is persistently knocking on the door. He has contaminated the creation and feels he can apply pressure on God because of the influence he holds. "Give me the keys to the kingdom or destroy the creation" were the last words I heard from Satan as he threatened God.

The platform given to Satan in this book is not one I enjoyed providing. It was difficult for me to write about the darkness that contaminates us all. However challenging it was to recount my interactions with Satan, including his attempts to kill me, I am committed to sharing the truth with all who seek it within these pages. With the completion of this chapter, we can now transition to a new phase of discussion—one that centers on the most incredible, loving, and creative (did I mention loving?) Father to ever exist. I am thrilled to share with you my experiences of walking in the love and presence of our Father, God, The Creator of the Universe.

The Path of Revelation to God's Heart

Before delving into the revelations of different things that God has disclosed, I would like to share a couple of short stories about the wonders of the human mind. This will help set the tone and understanding for a couple of revelations that will follow.

After having guided someone through a session, they shared an experience that seemed extraordinary, causing them to hesitate to share it. With a bit of encouragement, they began to reveal their earliest memory. They described being in their mother's womb when suddenly everything turned red, and they felt intense suffering. They remembered asking, "Why don't you want me? Why are you trying to kill me?" This experience represented the ultimate rejection from a parent. The person's mother had taken pills in an attempt to abort them.

During sessions conducted properly, individuals often dig into the deepest parts of their being. However, many of them struggle to share their experiences afterward because of the profound sensitivity they feel. One fear they have in sharing openly is the fear of rejection. They are concerned about being perceived as crazy. One particular difficulty people face is confessing their earliest memories. Why? This is because of the age at which these memories are recalled, memories from the womb, and even memories at birth. The concept of remembering events from such an early age is incomprehensible for the conscious mind. However, these memories are imprinted in the human mind because of traumatic events.

Initially, even I was cautious about accepting these accounts of early memories. However, these stories continued to emerge from independent individuals who had no connection to one another. These people didn't know each other, yet they shared remarkably similar experiences. One person recalled experiencing rejection while in the womb, recalling instances of their parents' fights and the realization that their father didn't want them. The father rejected the mother for being pregnant again. This had led to this person's trauma of rejection even before entering the world! It became clear that as soon as the brain is formed; it starts recording information. This information remains there today, even if you're not consciously aware of it, which leads me to the next story.

This lady had undergone approximately 8 sessions and had already worked through a significant amount. It was a struggle for her to come to terms with many of the memories that surfaced, but she had persisted in reaching this point. In this session, it was time for her to confront an incident that occurred when she was 18 years old, during a party. Even during the session, the memories were hazy because of her having been drugged and then abused. She witnessed the entire evening unfold before her, even though the memories were faint. This lady resisted what she saw repeatedly until finally; she remembered and accepted that it had happened. First, this illustrates a crucial aspect of the healing process: acceptance. We must accept that something has happened to us before we can release it. If we choose to deny, deny, deny and bury our heads in the sand, the trauma remains within us, slowly poisoning our well-being.

What sets this story apart is that the incident occurred when she was 18 years old. She had no memory of it. The pain was so overwhelming that even at that age, the memory could become locked away, inaccessible to the conscious mind. This illustrates how deeply traumatic experiences can be concealed within us. Now, consider the potential for emotional or physical trauma experienced by a young child to similarly remain hidden from our awareness.

How do these stories tie into what you'll read next? These narratives delve into the remarkable capabilities of the human mind as a store-house of experiences. They highlight how the mind safeguards us from past wounds and traumas, acting as a shield. However, what we carry from our past significantly shapes our present. Much like a prism, it distorts our view of the current situation. The lens through which we perceive them taints our beliefs and perceptions today, influenced by our past experiences. Satan uses this to manipulate a lie into something you'll accept as truth.

Let's explore God's heart on some of the most divisive topics in our contemporary society:

Abortion: God unveiled His heart on this matter to me one day. There's so much anger and hate on both sides of this issue. The right claims they are defending babies, while the left asserts the impor-tance of choice. Yet, all of this is a mere surface distraction from the deeper reality.

Amidst this conflict, young mothers are suffering. God assured me that the babies are safe. They are all with Him. However, His concern lies with the hearts of the mothers who have undergone abortions. Satan led these mothers to take the life of their own child. Following this, Satan attempts to manipulate them with the darkness he has created. This darkness burdens these mothers, further separating them from God. For those burdened with guilt, how can they face God? And for those who harbor enough hate to take pride in their actions, how can they truly understand God's love?

For God, the issue isn't solely about the children; He protects them. His genuine concern is the damage inflicted upon the heart. The spiritual battle doesn't get much darker than the influence of dark-ness required to take one's own child's life. God's worry extends to the hearts of these mothers. They are the ones who need His grace and love the most. God accepts them as they are. No act, no deed, could ever drive them away from God's love and salvation. He desires for all His children to be united with Him. He accepts everyone that comes to Him with an open heart.

Homosexuality: This is another attack by Satan that deeply saddens God's heart. Generations are affected and torn apart by this. God created us out of love and we are meant to share that love. Our connections with those around us are vital. The strongest connection of all exists between a parent and a child, a bond that transcends the physical. This special bond is a spiritual connection, and Satan seeks to destroy and sever it.

One of Satan's strategies to break the parental bond involves homosexuality. A specific demon is assigned the task of promoting homosexuality. Their goal is to influence individuals towards same-sex connections. This often begins with the parents, where some form of abuse, neglect, or rejection occurs. As a consequence of this pain, hatred may develop towards the father or mother. For example, a son might harbor such intense resentment towards his mother that he struggles to form healthy relationships with women. Similarly, a same-sex individual might enter the picture, offering solace amidst their shared suffering. These events can transpire at an early age or beyond the individual's conscious awareness.

Satan's aim is to sever the family's generational connections for the future. His attack not only targets the individual but also extends to the great-grandparents, grandparents, and parents of those affected. Consider a scenario where, out of just these three generations, totaling twelve individuals, 50% have embraced God and are spending eternity in heaven. However, the unfortunate outcome is that those six individuals already in with God will not have any more descendants to welcome into heaven. The family lineage has been eternally disrupted and cut off by Satan's influence.

God loves those who are facing Satan's attacks without wavering. But there's an important choice we all have to make. It's about choosing either God or Satan, and this choice becomes final when we take our very last breath. We don't know exactly when that will be, but it's a guarantee that it will happen. Just as with any sin, we cannot claim to walk in the light while residing in darkness.

1 John 1:5-6: *"This is the message we have heard from him and declare to you: God is light; in him, there is no darkness at all. If we claim to have fellowship with him and yet walk in the darkness, we lie and do not live out the truth."*

Choosing God

We've all chosen people to be with, whether a spouse, a significant other, or a friend. How many are still best friends with the person they knew at 8 years old? How many don't have any friends from 10 years ago? Relationships require energy and effort to maintain the connection. Divorced? Breakup? Not as close as you once were to your best friend? What led to these changes? What forces pulled you away from each other?

During my upbringing, the belief of 'Once saved, always saved' was a recurring theme in various churches. Do you recall those constant spiritual attacks I mentioned earlier in the book where I repeatedly chose God? It often led to frustration, and I couldn't help but cry out, 'Why, God? Why do I have to keep making this choice when I've already committed myself to You?' The answer to this perplexing question wouldn't become clear to me until much later, and regrettably, it was revealed through experiences involving close friends.

Some friends of mine had recently accepted God in their lives. Overflowing with joy and newfound love, their lives became brighter. They were always eager to share the new developments in their lives. Yet, as new believers, the foundation of their faith was still taking shape. Satan, relentless and competitive, couldn't stand to lose anyone to God. The attacks began immediately, often through their partners. If they were single, someone new would appear, seemingly perfect but not aligned with God. The intense attraction that was formed between them was coordinated by demons, a topic we've discussed before.

Soon, happiness became an attachment through these relationships, overshadowing the importance of growing closer to God or attending church to strengthen their faith with others. Instead, their partner would suggest connecting with God through nature or some other endeavor, an ever so slight detour with grave consequences. This was just one of Satan's methods for pulling people away from God. He employed various strategies to target individuals one by one.

After enduring countless attacks and repeatedly crying out to God, I finally understood the truth: **Choosing God is a continuous and ongoing decision**. Just as we need to invest energy into our daily relationships here on earth to maintain a strong connection with our loved ones, we must also do the same with our relationship with God. James 4:8 says, *'Come close to God, and God will come close to you.'* 1 Chronicles 22:19 also emphasizes the importance of continuously choosing God: *'Now seek the Lord your God with all your heart and soul.'*

If the truth was 'once saved, always saved,' then why would Satan launch attacks to pull the saved away from God? It would be akin to a baserunner in baseball safely reaching home plate and then strolling into the dugout to take a seat. Why would the opposing team rush into the dugout to try and tag him out if the umpire had already declared him safe?

Satan's strategy involves pulling people away from God, but the deception arises from the belief that they are eternally saved merely because they once accepted God. Unfortunately, this misconception has infiltrated some churches as well. Just like any relationship, you must nurture it; otherwise, it will inevitably fade into obscurity.

Matthew 7:21 *"Not everyone who calls out to me, 'Lord! Lord!' will enter the Kingdom of Heaven. Only those who actually do the will of my Father in heaven will enter."*

God conveyed to me, *"My people must choose me every second, of every minute, of every hour, of every day, of every week, of every month, of every year, of every decade, until they come home to me."* If not, Satan will find a way to creep back in and separate you from God. Nothing brings Satan more joy than stealing God's children away. How are you nurturing your relationship with God? In prayer? Seeking His will for your life? Choose Him always and forever, choose God.

The Tears of a Loving Creator

Months after the attack that nearly claimed my life, I nursed a grudge against God. Sure, He saved me from the hail of bullets that tore through the vehicle, but did He ever consider the aftermath of living with PTSD? Leaving the safety of my house became a struggle as I grappled with feelings of insecurity everywhere I went. The once-present joy in my life vanished, replaced by a persistent state of hyper-vigilance. Even my nightly walks with God, moments of intimate conversation and learning about His creation, felt like a distant memory. The darkness of night had turned into a threat, as I dreaded the insecurity of being in public spaces.

In a twisted way, it seemed like a win-win situation for Satan. He didn't take God's son away, but he clipped his wings. These are the natural scars etched into the human psyche by the touch of trauma. Although my healing was remarkably swift, it took months to uproot the deeply ingrained consequences from my mind.

Around three months later, drowning in a sea of self-pity because nothing seemed to restore my sense of normalcy, I privately confronted God with a question: "Why didn't you shield me from that attack? Could you not have prevented it?" After months of blaming Him, God's patience reached its limit.

God's voice was clear and, in that moment, He told me; *"I am not responsible for the attack. Satan targeted you. He is the sole one to bear the blame. There is no trace of evil within me; I refuse to shoulder that responsibility any longer."* His words hit me like a jolt. I was shocked!

"But, but, but, you are God. Responsibility falls on you," I stammered, my voice barely audible, a twinge of embarrassment creeping in. It was more of an audible thought than a statement of fact. He responded:

"I am tired of being blamed for the evil that takes place on this earth. This is what the people have chosen. It was never my intention to have a world with Satan in it. It was never the original design to see my people suffer like this. I am not responsible for the bad and the suffering on this earth. Only Satan is."

God's words are more than just words; they carry the weight of His emotions within them. There's no haziness; you can feel the presence and emotion in His words. His sadness at being blamed for the world's evil is unmistakable. It pained me to witness the weight that God carries to sustain the creation.

Satan has convinced the world that God is to blame for all the wrongs. In fact, the world has turned against God because of Satan's deceptive influence on people's minds. "Look at that war!" Satan whispers. "What kind of God would allow that? And look at that violence! If He really exists, He's insensible," the whispers continue, slowly creating a resentment in the hearts of man. Little by little, generation after generation, these whispers turn people away from a loving Father because of the lies and deceit that Satan spreads among God's creation.

God: Returning to Our Source

The God you know, isn't God. "Well, you can't possibly know this," you might be thinking. Yes, I can, because I too once knew God in the flesh, but now I have known Him in the spirit. The God I knew, the one who came into the five-year-old boy and protected him, is a loving God. We all know about the saving God, the God full of love, grace, and mercy; the God that saves from sin. One of the most famous hymns of all time is "Amazing Grace."

Amazing grace! How sweet the sound
That saved a wretch like me!
I once was lost, but now am found;
Was blind, but now I see.

How about some of the contemporary Christian music we've heard? Here is a well-known song by Casting Crowns called 'Who Am I':

Who am I, that the Lord of all the earth would care to know my name?
Would care to feel my hurt?
Who am I, that the bright and morning star would choose to light the way
For my ever wandering heart?

Not because of who I am
But because of what you've done
Not because of what I've done
But because of who you are
I am a flower quickly fading

Here today and gone tomorrow
A wave tossed in the ocean
A vapor in the wind....

Or another immensely popular song by the wonderful group Hillsong Worship: 'Who You Say I Am':

Who am I that the highest King
Would welcome me?
I was lost but He brought me in
Oh, His love for me
Oh, His love for me

Who the Son sets free
Oh, is free indeed
I'm a child of God
Yes, I am

Free at last, He has ransomed me
His grace runs deep
While I was a slave to sin
Jesus died for me
Yes, He died for me

These are all great songs that are representative of mankind's relationship with God. A Savior, a Rescuer, and a Protector for those of us who have accepted Him into our lives and seek His guidance. That's who we perceive God to be, but that's not the complete picture of who God truly Is.

Because of Satan's influence in the flesh, he can contaminate how we perceive God. My personal view was of a loving God who rescues people, but also a fierce judge. I saw God seated in heaven, looking down on Earth, judging every move and action. Guilt would overcome me when I sinned. I would berate myself for my mistakes and worry that God was looking down on me with disappointment.

This image of a perfect, judgmental, and authoritative high-ruling God was constantly present within me. The notion that everything occurring on Earth is God's will because He exercises control and dominion over everything prevailed. Why would God permit children to be murdered at schools? How can a good God be responsible for children born with defects? What kind of God permits innocent people to fall victim to violent crime? If God is in control, why do such evil things happen?

In this way, Satan tarnishes our perception of God from within. For many, this distortion becomes so profound that they outright reject God because of the suffering they've endured. Some even deny God's existence altogether. After all, who would willingly embrace a deity who allows such terrible evils to persist? Ultimately, Satan succeeds in convincing most individuals to attribute the suffering we endure to God.

Even for those who have embraced God as their loving Father, this contamination alters how we are able to perceive God. Those who accept God view Him through a lens of distortion influenced by Satan. Why? Because we are human, and two spiritual forces are constantly at work within us. Regardless of whether you perceive or are conscious of it, the ongoing battle is being waged by both sides. Only when we depart from this earth, will we be liberated from Satan's influence and finally able to see God in His true essence. He is the Greatest and most Magnificent existence I have ever encountered in my solitary life. Next, I will share my personal encounters with our loving Father.

The Unveiling:
My First Encounter with God

At this juncture in my profound healing journey, God had already healed all my pain, and I was gradually gaining deeper insights into the spirit. On one occasion, the Holy Spirit spoke to me as though He were a person standing right beside me. "God wants to reveal Himself to you. He wants you to understand that it will forever change your perspective of Him. Whoever sees God is changed forever. Considering the profound implications of what is about to transpire, do you consent to God revealing Himself to you?" What! A chance to see more of God? To know Him more intimately? Absolutely!

I was filled with eager anticipation. I sensed that something huge was being unveiled to me. Expecting to be embraced by a love that was beyond my comprehension, accompanied by beautiful sensations and feelings of happiness. However, what I began to feel and see was nothing like that. The revelation that unfolded before me was far from anything I ever imagined. In fact, it contradicted who I had thought God to be. It left me utterly humbled and speechless.

I felt an intense vulnerability coming from God. A sense of pureness untouched by any blemish. A sensitivity like I had never known before. Comparing it to the innocence and vulnerability of a small child couldn't even begin to capture its depth; it was as if that innocence was multiplied by a thousand. Suddenly, I understood the nature of my sensitive heart. I understood why harsh words and yelling hurt me so deeply. I had my Father's heart.

God's sweet, pure, innocent, and naked vulnerability was before me, and I sensed His shyness in exposing all of that to me. It was as though He dreaded my potential rejection once I saw who He is. This level of vulnerability, which I had never felt before in my life, left me speechless. I began crying, seeing this revelation of who God is.

The encounter forever changed me. For days afterward, I moved around like a zombie, deeply impacted by the realization of who God truly is. Assimilating what I had witnessed and felt was a challenge beyond words. Slowly, I began to understand that we are all likenesses of our Father. He isn't solely a mighty ruler, judge, and Savior. He's so much more. My words can't even begin to capture His essence. They actually have the opposite effect; these words rob Him of the true nature of who our Creator is.

This would be only the first of many revelations about who our Father really is, each revelation a distinct and powerful experience that would leave me speechless every time. Join me as we continue to explore our God and Father in the next chapter.

God's Unexpected Laughter: Seeing His Humor

During one of my evening walks, God was teaching me about the creation. I Inquired about the possibility of having a spouse, and God's response was, *"I won't send you one now; I have work for you to do. Oh, and don't expect Satan to send you anybody either! Hahaha."* I found this quite funny, as I instantly grasped that anyone who came close to me had their demons exposed. No way Satan wanted that! Initially, I dismissed it as my ego laughing at the notion, since an almighty God surely couldn't possess a sense of humor, right? Little did I know what was about to unfold.

A short while later, as I prepared for a session, I sensed the urge to invite a friend over to assist me with a massage pistol during the session. Prior to this, we had discovered that the vibrations of a massage pistol significantly aided somatic releases. This helped effectively disperse trapped darkness (energy) from the body. I had a feeling that something significant was approaching, and the vibrations would be instrumental in facilitating the release.

This session involved the continual removal of demons. While in the middle of it, I sensed an immense fear coming from the demons, as they dreaded the prospect of God using the massage pistol against them. They trembled at the idea of my friend being summoned to assist. There was a constant dread with the question, 'when is the pistol coming? When is the pistol coming?'

And then, in an extraordinary display of His incredible, loving, and profoundly humorous nature, I felt the presence of God envelop me, His power washing over me. What followed was a pure, divine laughter that I didn't know even existed. God's laughter erupted, resonating with joy and directed at the trembling demons, fearing the massage pistol.

His laughter proved infectious, and my friend in the living room soon found herself laughing uncontrollably upon hearing it. *"They're so foolish!"* God exclaimed. *"What did they believe? That God couldn't remove demons before the invention of the massage pistol? Hahaha, lol."* In good humor, He continued, *"Apologies, but I can't assist you at the moment. It's 1890, and I'll need another 100 years before I can rid you of these demons. Hahaha, lol."* His playful jokes continued to resonate.

God's laughter and playful jokes carried on. *"God, the demon remover since 1990! Hahaha, what do they think?"* He chuckled, *"I need a massage pistol to get rid of them?"* His pure divine laughter continued for perhaps 15 minutes. Tears streamed down my face as the moments unfolded. When a demon emerged for removal, God joined in with a lighthearted remark, *"Hold on... give me a moment... I'm searching for my massage pistol... now, where did I put it? Hahaha."* After sharing a good laugh at the expense of the demons, He promptly removed them. Amid his laughter, He said to me, *"Son, sometimes you just have to find laughter in the little things, even if nobody else comprehends it."* Maybe it was just a special moment shared between us that nobody will comprehend, but it was so special to see our Father in that way. Never in my life did I think that the Creator of the universe had a sense of humor like that!

Our Father understands us far more than we know. When I felt hurt by others, that was a trait of our Father. When I laughed, that was a trait of our Father. When I felt angry at injustices, that was a trait of our Father. When I showed love to others, that was a trait of our Father. When I showed patience, that was a trait of our Father. When

I showed mercy, that was a trait of our Father. When I created something, that was a trait of our Father. In the days that followed these events, after decades on this earth, I finally understood the meaning of Genesis 1:27: *"So God created mankind in his own image, in the image of God he created them…"*

Embracing the Spirit:
Unveiling God's Truth

-John 4:24, *"God is spirit, and his worshipers must worship in the Spirit and in truth."*

-1 Corinthians 2:14, *"The person without the Spirit does not accept the things that come from the Spirit of God but considers them foolishness, and cannot understand them because they are discerned only through the Spirit."*

-Ephesians 1:17, *"I keep asking that the God of our Lord Jesus Christ, the glorious Father, may give you the Spirit of wisdom and revelation, so that you may know him better."*

-1 Corinthians 6:17, *"But whoever is united with the Lord is one with him in spirit."*

We understand God could no longer walk on the earth with us once Satan was invited in. This event was deeply sorrowful for Him, as His longing to be with His creation endures to this very day. What is happening to His people weighs heavily on His heart. He has conveyed to me with unwavering emphasis that *"Nothing else matters but the hearts of my people."* Above all other concerns, His utmost priority is to reach the hearts of each individual on this planet, offering them the opportunity of choice. Every person on this earth will encounter this choice in their lifetime. God has assured me that no individual will leave this earthly existence without the chance to choose God above all else. They have the freedom to choose, but He makes sure they have that choice.

We can only encounter God in the realm of the spirit. His divine nature prevents Him from inhabiting the earth directly. This revelation unfolded when God drew close to me on one occasion. Amidst a chorus of voices exclaiming, "No, God! Don't do it! Come back, God!" I also urgently told Him, "No, God, you must protect the divinity." The concept of God's divinity had seldom crossed my mind, but that day, it was unveiled before me.

Satan's presence within the creation acts like a contamination, a cancer that corrodes everything it touches. Upon Satan's entry into the creation, it forced God to depart. An army protects God's purity, His divinity. Their sole mission is to shield His divinity from Satan. I was shown that if Satan were to reach God, he would taint His purity, leading to the annihilation of the entire creation—both earthly and heavenly. God's existence would cease to be.

Satan's relentless aim, his very purpose, is to reach God. He aspires to displace Him from His throne and take over the kingdom. This is why he relentlessly destroys the creation. His intent is to lure God into the creation, within his reach, and defile His divinity. A couple of weeks after this revelation, I felt compelled to read the Book of Revelation, a biblical text I hadn't explored in over three decades, dismissing it as too complex to decipher. Within its pages, I encountered a passage that resonated deeply with the revelation given to me.

Revelation 12:7-8 and verse 12 state:

"Then there was war in heaven. Michael and his angels fought against the dragon and his angels. And the dragon lost the battle, and he and his angels were forced out of heaven. This great dragon—the ancient serpent called the devil, or Satan, the one deceiving the whole world—was thrown down to the earth with all his angels.

Therefore, rejoice, O heavens! And you who live in the heavens, rejoice! But terror will come on the earth and the sea, for the devil has come down to you in great anger, knowing that he has little time."

This passage confirms what God revealed to me: Satan's purpose is to get to Him. I also understood why those who live in the heavens should rejoice. If Satan could reach God, it would spell the destruction of the entire creation, including heaven. This realization was in line with what I saw when Satan demanded, "Give me the keys to the kingdom" from God.

It's clear from the book of Revelation that Satan plans to mount an attack to seize control of the entire creation from God. This sets the stage for our exploration of a message of hope from God in the next chapter.

Faith and Hope: A Message to His People

The human mind is limited, designed to protect us on this earth and shield us from the full knowledge of the spiritual war raging within us every day. In fact, the more that evil is accepted in a society, the lower the consciousness of its people becomes. God is compelled to lower the consciousness of His children in such a society because if they were to see the truth of the evil surrounding them, it could be devastating. Their will to live would be significantly diminished. Happiness would be nonexistent among them. The only way to find happiness amidst evil is by remaining mostly unaware of its presence.

This is why societies in third-world countries, where evil has been accepted on a greater scale, are more dangerous but also possess a notably lower overall level of consciousness. There is real-world evidence of this in overall IQ scores taken from different countries. You could correlate the IQ scores with the crime rate of that country to observe the relationship. I am not here to judge, only to present the truth of what is. Accepting this truth is extremely challenging for some; nonetheless, it is the truth.

We live our entire lives surrounded by eternity, yet most are not even conscious of it. One night, as I sat on my couch, God began to teach me. He directed my gaze to the night sky and whispered, *"That is eternity."* Looking upward at the stars illuminating the night sky, my eyes were opened, and it left me speechless. All my life, I lived within the embrace of eternity, an endless existence, yet struggled to grasp its concept.

God has created an eternal place for those who choose Him. A place free from darkness and death. A place without time, suffering, and the trials of this life. A place built from love, where your wealth is your heart, not your bank account. A place where you will be in the presence of God's pure, divine love for eternity.

John 14:2-3 *"My Father's house has many rooms; if that were not so, would I have told you that I am going there to prepare a place for you? And if I go and prepare a place for you, I will come back and take you to be with me that you also may be where I am."*

2 Corinthians 5:1 *"For we know that if the earthly tent we live in is destroyed, we have a building from God, an eternal house in heaven, not built by human hands."*

1 Peter 1:3-4 *"Praise be to the God and Father of our Lord Jesus Christ! In his great mercy he has given us new birth into a living hope through the resurrection of Jesus Christ from the dead, and into an inheritance that can never perish, spoil or fade. This inheritance is kept in heaven for you."*

The faith we hold in God and the hope for a future free from the suffering of this world are important messages from God that we must guard in our hearts, if we choose to do so.

Two Paths: Just Choose

"All my people have to do is choose." This is the simple desire of God. He pleads with us to make a choice, and His impatience grows with those who don't. Frustration is evident in God's heart towards those who fail to choose. People's decision to not choose and to live a life of 70, 80, or 90-plus years places God in a challenging position. The consequences of those who do not choose force those who have chosen God to endure longer suffering. There are many factors to this decision that God has revealed during our time together.

The most challenging aspect involves the sons, daughters, grandsons, and granddaughters of the people in heaven. They implore God to extend the timeline of the creation so that their offspring will have more time to choose the path leading to God. If God were to end the creation today, a lot of those in heaven would lose a son or a daughter for eternity. The pain of that loss is incredibly difficult for God to accept. Older generations in heaven would have entire families with them, leaving the last generation alone with very few sons and daughters. God listens to the pleas of those with Him and grants their sons and daughters more time to choose.

However, granting them time to choose gives rise to another issue. Those on earth who have chosen God continue to suffer in this world. This causes God to experience a deep anguish, witnessing His children endure the attacks of the enemy for the sake of those who haven't chosen yet. His love is so profound that He continually postpones judgment for the sake of those who might still choose to be with Him. Consider the example of adults who decide to be with

God at the age of 50. Had He judged the earth when they were 35, their eternal life would have been tormented in hell. Now, they can be with God in His love for all eternity. This is the relentless struggle that God faces every millisecond of every second, of every minute, of every hour and of every day.

We do not know what God endures to hold the universe together. Let's express our gratitude to Him. Offer praises and prayers to God. Encourage Him with words of support. Just like us, He feels and experiences emotions. He endures anguish and feels the weight of His creation. Let's thank God for His true nature. Let's appreciate Him for successfully maintaining the universe's harmony in the face of constant attacks. Show Him your gratitude. Even if you're going through a difficult phase or suffering, remember that it would be unfathomably worse without God's protection. Take a moment to express your gratitude to Him today.

The Power of Prayer:
God's Connection to Us

W e were created to exist independently of God's will. This is the essence of true free will: a people designed for autonomy from God. Think of a renowned painter and his artworks. Each one bears a unique image, yet they all carry something distinctive. A painter can't create a painting without leaving a trace of who they are. Every painter has a trademark style or story embedded in their work.

This is the true brilliance of God's creation of us. Each of us is different, yet independent of the Artist who created us. We are each crafted to be autonomous from the Creator, a genuine masterpiece of creativity. So how was this achieved? Apart from the spirit, a mechanism was designed to function independently of God: the mind. It was created to preserve each individual body it is connected to, to the best of its ability.

Have you ever found yourself pondering the intricate workings of the human mind, wondering about the origins of its thoughts and the deeper spiritual and physical implications that underlie our mental processes? If so, you're not alone in your quest for understanding. Many have embarked on a similar journey, delving into the realms of philosophy and spirituality. Now, let's circle back to the fundamental question: What does all of this have to do with the act of prayer?

If you recall, we discussed how both God and Satan have a place within us. Can you guess where in the body God reserves for Himself? Yep, the heart. God's presence within us envelops the organ that pumps life into the body. Many people testify that when they accept God, they feel a warm sensation in their chest, confirming that something significant has just occurred. That is God fully enveloping the area around the heart. He no longer has to stand at the door; He has been invited in.

So, the mind is inherently self-preserving and primarily focused on its own interests, as it was designed to be. On the other hand, the heart is the source of love and selflessness. It's where considerations for others' needs and concerns originate. Even if you haven't fully embraced God, you were created from Him, and a fragment of His love lives within you.

Prayer serves to align the mind with the heart, syncing these two vital organs and creating a connection within us. This alignment of the mind with the heart allows God to work within the world. He then has access to the mind, which directs the body. God's love can direct the person to take the correct course of action in a certain situation. Influence the mind to show kindness to someone in need or to bless someone through your actions. Prayer functions as an open channel through which God's presence can flow into the world, shaping our actions and interactions with His wisdom and love.

Now, consider this: What if the mind is stronger than the heart? In that case, your prayers might revolve around asking God for things that the mind was created to handle, such as personal protection, financial blessings, and health. Seeking to connect to God through self-centered means. But what if the heart is stronger than the mind? In this scenario, your prayers will still seek these same blessings, but with a focus on others as well. You'll be asking for God's blessings, not just for yourself, but also for the well-being of others. It's a shift from an inward focus, which characterizes the mind's perspective, to an outward focus which represents the heart's capacity for love.

Together in Prayer: Amplifying God's Power through Unity

Mathew 18:19-20, *"I also tell you this: If two of you agree here on earth concerning anything you ask, my Father in heaven will do it for you. For where two or three gather together as my followers, I am there among them."*

People coming together in prayer creates a powerful connection with God. Because of the contamination of sin in the world, God's presence has been removed from the creation. His power on this earth lives in each one of us. Every human has a small part of God, our Father, dwelling within. Remember, the spiritual connection exists within us, not floating in the surrounding air. God is connected to the heart of every human born into this world.

Recently, I experienced strong somatic releases and decided it would be best to lie down. I was coughing relentlessly, as if removing something large from my body, and tasted blood. My mind tried to protect me, urging, 'That's enough.' Then, a voice said, 'Do you not think your Creator knows what you can handle?' In that moment, a pure white light flashed by on my left side. My lungs filled to their maximum capacity, and my body locked up, as if I were in a scene from a movie where they shock a person with electricity to restart the heart. Filled with terror, I hid my face in the pillow and curled up in a ball on the bed. God had just passed by. With my eyes closed, I could feel my entire left side bathed in pure white energy, unlike anything I had ever experienced before. The mere passing of God had left me 'burned' with His divinity. God's power is absolutely indescribable, beyond words.

It filled me with alarm for days after God passed by, and I still feel a sense of distress that it might happen again, to the point where I've even asked Him for a warning if it does, haha. I fully comprehend that if I had been in God's presence for even one second longer, it would have meant instant death for me. His power is so immense that we cannot endure His full presence. So, considering God's overwhelming power, why is there a need for more power through unity in prayer? These are complex concepts to grasp with the mind, but I'll do my best to explain, praying that the intended explanation is understood.

Since God's full presence cannot inhabit the Earth, He has placed small amounts of Himself in every one of us. Those who have opened their hearts and accepted God have a stronger presence of His light and love within them. This is how God guides the direction of life, through His presence in all of us. So, when we come together as a group to pray and connect with one another, God's presence on Earth is stronger through the shared connection in all of us.

The Bible emphasizes the importance of prayer in our daily life:

Ephesians 6:18 *"Pray in the Spirit at all times and on every occasion. Stay alert and be persistent in your prayers for all believers everywhere."*

Philippians 4:6-7 *"Don't worry about anything; instead, pray about everything. Tell God what you need, and thank him for all he has done. Then you will experience God's peace, which exceeds anything we can understand. His peace will guard your hearts and minds as you live in Christ Jesus."*

James 5:16 *"Confess your sins to each other and pray for each other so that you may be healed. The earnest prayer of a righteous person has great power and produces wonderful results."*

As times grow darker and life becomes more challenging, it becomes even more crucial for people to unite in prayer. Only through this shared connection, which allows God to flow through us with greater power, can He protect His people in the darkest of hours. This unity will be absolutely critical for the times that lie ahead in the creation. Come together and pray. Remember these words; they are from your Father.

To God's Children: Embracing the Path of Faith and Hope

A uthor's note: I was starting the chapter with the above title when God's spirit came over me, and He began dictating a message directly for His people. This is that message:

"I am a God of love. I do not harm you. My children, listen to my words and heed my warnings. I have allowed this creation to continue because of my love for you. My love extends to the farthest regions of this earth. There is no one that my love can't reach. Be faithful, love one another, and show the world my love through your kindness. I know the pain suffered by this world. I see the acts of Satan beneath the sun. Nothing is hidden from me. Live in the faith that I will protect you. I will seek vengeance for wrong done against my children that have chosen me. No act against my people will be done without judgment.

I am a God that sees all and knows the hearts of all my people. Do not be fooled by the guidance of those around you. Do not open yourselves to the deception of the enemy. The father of darkness is all around you. Do not let him in. It would be better for you to perish immediately in this world then fall victim to Satan's lies and deceit.

My message is a message of hope to the ones that will hear my voice. Do not look for rewards in this life. The only way to obtain rewards in this life is to live in this world. This world has been destroyed by the prince of darkness. Only darkness seeks success in this world that is lost to its desires. My children, follow my words and keep my commands. This is the only way to eternal life. No one is exempt from this. Many people have been lost in this life thinking they were holy or wise in my ways. Do not be foolish, for your mind knows nothing of what this life is offering you.

I have come to warn you. A time is near when this earth will erupt and spit out the evil at its core. I have commanded the earth to reject its urge to fight against the darkness. It will allow what is to come, to come. A time is coming when the earth won't feel my presence in it. A darkness will come over the land and engulf it. To my believers, I have sent angels to protect you. You will feel the pressures of this world against you, but I will protect you from imminent destruction.

Have hope, my children. This is what will get you through the times that are coming. Hope that your father will rescue you. Hope that this is done to bring a better life for those that choose it. A hope for your children to come to me. I will tolerate the sins of this world no more. The people have made their choices, now they will endure the final days. Keep your heads up and your spirit clean. Do not fall into the pit that devours.

My hand will guide you. Follow me to avoid capture by the enemy. Few will know me in these times, but many are waiting for you in heaven. A special place is waiting for you here with me for those who endure what is to come. These are my final words. Listen, you who will listen. Mercy to the ones who ignore my words and follow the beast into the pit of death. Unite with one another in my love so that you may endure the final days".

This word came to me as I was writing the book, Final Truth. It is being written for the people that will listen. These words cannot be changed, for these are the words of God for which He has spoken through me. Anyone who dares to manipulate these final words of God meant for His creation will be held accountable by the Most High.

Final Thoughts: Walking with God

As I embarked on the last section of this book, I realized God had a closing message, a word of hope and warning meant for His people. This revelation came unexpectedly, a realization that His words needed to be captured verbatim. I, a mere conduit for His words, found myself humbled and awed by the weight of His message. There was no room for my interpretation, no place for any embellishments. His words, pure and profound, stood alone, for the hearts that would listen.

When I initially sat down to pen what I thought would be a concise Facebook post, little did I know that a torrent of words would spill out, an outpouring that defied expectation. The last book, a labor of five months, spanned 21,000 words in its preliminary draft. Remarkably, the pages of this new endeavor have swelled to 33,000 words in the brief span of 14 days. This is the manifestation of the Spirit's power, the embodiment of a message authored by God, a message with the potential to reshape lives, if only it reaches receptive ears and open hearts.

Consider this: what I share is not solely my doing, but a testimony to the workings of God's love for His people. As you read these lines with your eyes and grapple with comprehension through your mind, remember that their true understanding lies in the spirit. Look beyond the mere text and search your heart. Free yourself from the constraints of the mind and let the Spirit carry you to realms where God's guidance flows freely. Strive to attune yourself to His voice, to become a vessel through which God can reach others.

During the stillness of your moments with God, mend the lingering pain within you. As you heal and release the darkness, God's presence can transform you in ways you might have never thought possible in this lifetime. In these times, the world needs individuals who are deeply connected to God, those who respond to His voice with open hearts. As your relationship grows with God, His voice in you becomes a radiant beacon of light. A light that cuts through the shadows of the lives of those around you with an unprecedented love and brilliance.

As you turned the pages, you had a choice. You could have let the words remain on the surface of your thoughts, or you could have dived deep, allowing them to breathe life into the spirit within you. Those words were more than mere writing; they were truths you might not have previously recognized or been conscious of. Discovering God's truth isn't solely about understanding; it involves surrendering to the spirit and allowing God to guide you.

As this chapter concludes, remember that you're holding more than just words. You possess a fundamental truth that can liberate you, ease the burdens of your heart, and unveil a fresh path you may not yet be aware of. Let these words stay with you as time passes, serving as a constant reminder that you're never alone on your journey. God walks beside you, guiding the way, and patiently waiting for your acceptance.

To all my brothers and sisters who have journeyed alongside me until now, I extend my heartfelt gratitude. Thank you for seeking the truth and walking this path with unwavering curiosity. The truth isn't always easy to accept, but God has illuminated it for us to decide which path to choose. Remember, God is by your side, loving you, and recognizing you as His own.

Stay steadfast and continue progressing towards God and His purpose for your life. Keep the flame of hope burning within, so you'll be ready at the end of this earthly journey, prepared for the next chapter that awaits you in the heavens. I eagerly anticipate the day we come together in heavenly worship, sharing in the love that awaits beyond this world's horizon.

May God's blessings envelope you, and with abundant love,

Sincerely,

Justin.

Epilogue

Before starting this book, God led me to the 'Bible belt' to ensure my safety from Satan's attacks. While serving in Mexico, God told me He could no longer guarantee my safety there because of Satan's significant influence. The attack that nearly left me dead was a sign of how Satan can launch attacks from the darkness and God has to rapidly respond to them. Leaving behind the orphanages and my friends was heart-wrenching, but I am committed to following God's will to the end. Upon arriving here, I immediately sensed a change in the spiritual atmosphere. The people here radiate more light, and there are many churches surrounding me. It's been refreshing to be among some of the friendliest people I've encountered in a long time.

This book is undeniably a miracle. Satan has made two attempts on my life in the last 11 months, with the most recent attempt occurring just last night. During a break from finishing up on the second draft, I went for my customary walk before sunset. I cherish my walks with God in the countryside, where we engage in meaningful conversations, allowing me to clear my mind of the world's distractions.

I have a preferred country road, free of traffic, where I take my walks. On average, I encounter only two to three passing cars during a one-hour walk. The area boasts scenic hills all around, and I felt safer here, knowing that God placed me in this location for my protection. I started to believe that life might return to 'normal' now that I've distanced myself from the powerful influence of Satan.

I was on my way back in the evening when I noticed headlights approaching from behind. It's a small country road, maybe one and a half lanes wide. I was walking in the middle and shifted to the left to be on the shoulder of the oncoming lane. Suddenly, God told me to move to the right side of the roadway. So, I crossed back over and stood about three feet off the road just before the vehicle approached.

As it drew close to me, I heard a loud thud and the screeching of metal. Sparks illuminated the roadway, and a truck passed by, with a detached trailer right behind it, traveling at about 35-40 mph. The separated trailer veered into the oncoming portion of the roadway and rode down the shoulder before crashing into the ditch and flying into the air, spilling its contents everywhere.

I was absolutely shocked because the disconnected trailer had traveled down the portion of the shoulder where I had been walking. On my walk back home, I couldn't help but wonder, 'Did Satan just try to take me out again?' When I arrived home, I felt God's presence and knew He had a message for me.

"Son, I'm so, so, so sorry," God said. *"There are no accidents in the creation. The demons blinded the man to the issue with his trailer to harm you while you were on that stretch of the road."* I immediately thought back to God's stern warning to Satan that not even a hair on my head should be harmed, and God responded to that thought. *"I judged the demons for their actions against you, but Satan doesn't care how many he loses to remove you from the creation. He knows that my presence in you is an incredible threat and has convinced his followers to die, if necessary, to eliminate you from the creation."*

I felt a profound sorrow in God because His presence within the creation was provoking these attacks. However, I knew it was for a purpose. Then, He uttered words that both crushed me and illuminated the visions I had been experiencing. *"I don't know how long I can protect you from Satan,"* God admitted, and my heart sank. I grasped they meticulously planned these attacks in the darkness, concealed from God's view. While He knew about this attack and had warned me, the violent attack by gunfire that occurred 11 months earlier was already in progress before He rapidly intervened to protect me.

This burden weighs heavily on me today, the day after the second attack. I understand this book exposes the darkness, and it seems Satan will go to any lengths to silence the truth about his actions within the creation. In the 15 hours since this attack on me, there have been four other attacks on my friends. I have a deep inner sense that once my purpose of shining light into the world is fulfilled, I may be called home earlier than I had expected, not only to protect myself but also the loved ones around me.

Darkness is enveloping the creation at an unprecedented rate. With modern inventions, previously isolated cultures and individuals are now intermingling. The internet facilitates the rapid spread of hatred. Someone who harbored hate seventy years ago had few friends and minimal influence because people would distance themselves, isolating that negativity. However, today, that same individual can send messages and posts, spreading hatred to millions in an instant. This serves as just one example. Now, imagine that 50% of the population is interconnected daily, disseminating lies and deceit globally. It's a pandemic of darkness engulfing the creation.

Stay focused on God, for He knows that times will become even more challenging for His children. This tribulation is necessary to save as many people as possible. It's akin to squeezing the juice out of an orange. The pressure will be difficult for all involved, but it's the essential process of separating the good from the bad, extracting the juice from everything else that doesn't align with God's goodness.

Anyone who writes knows the value of having another set of eyes look over their work to ensure flow and proper grammar. God had given me explicit instructions that no other person could have access to this text written here. I, as the author, had to perform the developmental editing, content editing, copy editing, line editing, cover art and proofreading of this book to ensure its integrity wasn't compromised.

May God bless the lives of the people who open their hearts to Him. After witnessing the splendor and beauty of heaven, with millions upon millions of people worshiping God and feeling the overwhelming love that freely flows throughout, I can wholeheartedly assure each one of you that the fight, the struggle, and the trials of this life will unquestionably be worth what God has in store for you.

1 John 2:15-17, *"Do not love this world nor the things it offers you, for when you love the world, you do not have the love of the Father in you. For the world offers only a craving for physical pleasure, a craving for everything we see, and pride in our achievements and possessions. These are not from the Father, but are from this world. And this world is fading away, along with everything that people crave. But anyone who does what pleases God will live forever."*

www.ingramcontent.com/pod-product-compliance
Lightning Source LLC
Chambersburg PA
CBHW051829040426

42447CB00006B/444